The Journey To Peace

A Woman's Guide to Finding Inner Peace

Carol Lynne Watson

THE JOURNEY TO PEACE
A Woman's Guide to Finding Inner Peace
CAROL LYNNE WATSON

Published by Pecan Tree Publishing, April 2010
Hollywood, Fl.
www.pecantreepress.com

This book or parts thereof may not be reproduced in any form, stored in a retrieval system, or transmitted in any form by any means – electronic, mechanical, photocopy, recording, or otherwise – without prior written permission of the publisher, author or legal representative of both parties, except as provided by United States of America copyright law.

Copyright © 2010 by Carol Lynne Watson

Library of Congress Control Number: 2010924213

ISBN: 978-0-9821114-3-7

PECAN TREE PUBLISHING
Hollywood, Fl.

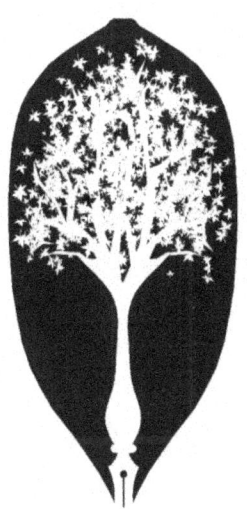

www.pecantreepress.com
New Voices | New Styles | New Vision

The Journey To Peace

Journey Hands Photography - Craig Stafford
Take Action and Prayer Photography - Angelica Velez
Interior Layout - Ann Steer

Table of Contents

Dedication iii
Acknowledgements iv
Foreword vii
One Day I'm Gonna Cry. viii
The Purpose of My Journey... xi

Journeys

1. My Journey Begins.... 21
2. Carol Watson, A Pleasure to Meet You, My Name Is Peace.... 26
3. A Good Place to Start... 28
4. Forgiveness... 31
5. The Source of Peace (How Well Do You Know Him?) 35
6. I Am Grateful... 38
7. Rid Yourself Of The Negatives... 41
8. Surround Yourself With Positives... 47
9. Faith on Your Journey.... 50
10. Visualize The Journey... 53
11. Find Your Peaceful Place... 56
12. Be Authentically You.... 58
13. Detours.... 62
14. Dance to Your Own Rhythm.... 66
15. Be Silly, Just For the Heck of It.... 69
16. Decide to Be the Bright Spot in Someone Else's Day and You Will Be Blessed For it..... 72
17. Practice Peace through Controlling Your Tongue.... 74

18. Find Pockets Of Peace Wherever You Can.... 77
19. Appreciate Yourself......................80
20. Make Peace (Or Live Peacefully) With Your Quirks.....................83
21. Redefine Yourself......................86
22. Peace Interrupted......................91
23. Peace Under Fire (Maintaining Your Grace)... 94
24. Enjoy The View........................97
25. Make Peace With The Knowledge That You May Have To Take Your Journey Alone..... 100
26. Determine Your Destination..............103
27. Practice Peace by Showing Compassion......106
28. Maintain Your Spiritual Health, It Is Essential To Your Journey..........109
29. Embrace Peace........................112
30. Expose Yourself........................115
31. Practice Peace by Showing Love..........118
32. Change Your Direction..................123
33. Live Simply..........................126
34. The Answers You Seek May Already Be Inside You....................129
35. Pray For Peace........................131
36. Our Journey Continues..................133
In the Moment..........................135

This book is dedicated to...
Louis James Maxwell (Jay)

John 15:13 says, *"Greater love has no one than this, that he lay down his life for his friends."*

Jay, you made this world a safer place. You are our hero, and you are missed. We love you and we are thankful to God for the 27 years He gave us with you.

For Michele and Giselle Vinas who left us too soon. This world was graced by your presence. You are loved and you are missed.

Acknowledgements

I have been blessed on my journey because amazing people surround me.

God, Thank You for loving 'even me'. I am grateful for the many gifts You have given me. I am especially grateful for the gift of Christ Jesus.

Charles and Janice Smith: Mommy and Daddy, thank you for always being so supportive of me. I love you both.

Lisa Janel Smith: Words cannot express the love and respect I have in my heart for you. You are not only my little sister; you are my best of best friends.

John, Travey and Janel: You guys are so awesome. It is such a pleasure being your mom. I love you.

Frantz and Jessie Noel: You guys are my family in every true sense of the word. I adore you both so much. Lots and lots of love to you.

Sharon Lawyer and Carlos Hall: My best friends of how many years? I love you both and I do not take for granted that you have always been there for me.

Michelle Whitehead: I love you Miso. I believe I have been waiting my whole life to meet you. Thank you for the view from the window.

Grandma Leasie: You are the treasure in our family. I love you.

Aunt Carolyn (Blake): Thank you for all the times you were there for me growing up. I have always looked up to you and I have always loved you. I will never forget the time you invested in me. Thank you so much. Love you, love you, and love you. (Don't tell Aunt Edith, but you are my favorite aunt)

Aunt Edith (Reeves): I have always admired your class and sassiness. You are one of my favorite people and I am so proud that you are my aunt. Thank you for being such a great role model to write about, and thanks for letting me share your story. I love you. (Don't tell Auntie Carolyn, but you are my favorite aunt)

Uncle Tommy (Smith): You make me laugh. You are one of my favorite people. I could have never replaced you in this family. I am glad you got a chance to see me come into this world on your way to Vietnam, but I am more grateful that you made it home safely. You are a jewel among men and I am glad you are my daddies little brother. I love you. I cannot wait to read your story. (Your favorite niece)

Denese, Robyn, Chantal, Craig, Tommie and Bobbie, Freeman Jr. and Donnie: I love you all. I am so happy that we are cousins.

Sabrina: I like knowing that even if we had not been cousins, we would still be friends. I love you. Thank you for always being in my corner. By the way, never was there a prettier bride.

Aunt Rosalind: Thank you for giving whatever you have to help whenever you can. Thank you for the time you spend with my kids. I love you Lala.

Auntie Audrey: I do not know how to express my feelings for you accurately. You came along and gave my uncle Freeman a brand new lease on life. You introduced him to love beyond what he had ever experienced. You have been his backbone at a time when he could have given up. You deserve more than this life has to offer and Heaven has many rewards waiting for you. Until then, I am so glad you are a part of this family. You are beautiful inside and out. I love you.

To my family in St. Louis: Dana, Nikki, Uncle Carl, Auntie Annette and Aunt Ginger. Love you guys.

Claudia Lewis: I love you and I treasure your friendship.

E. Claudette Freeman: My Editor, Publisher and Friend. Girl, this is it. All the times I had to tell God on you for making me do stuff I did not want to do. Oh yeah, by the way; thanks for making me do things I did not want to do. Peace as a character; who would have thought. God placed you in my path and I am blessed because of it.

My Church of The Holy Spirit Song family: Lots of love for you all.

Thank you all for taking this journey with me.

My journey has not been without its share of loss...

Mary Francis Kelley: I miss you Nana.

Granddaddy (Herman Kelley): Thank you for that last dance.

L.C. Smith: I miss you Papa.

Tasha Smalls: My little godchild. You did not deserve all the pain your body forced on you. I miss you sweetie but no more pain for you.

Allegra Bowens: This is hard for me to write. I miss you. You were my family in every true sense of the word. I cannot believe you are gone. I know you are in a better place, but I sure wish you were still here. Thank you for all the times you helped me with John when I was raising him as a single parent. You made me feel like I was not doing it alone. I wish I could have five minutes with you, because we have some unfinished thank you's and I love you's that I am not sure I said. If you can hear me girl, "Thank you." "I love you." God knows I miss you.

FOREWORD

It was a simple and easy Saturday afternoon. I had been invited to share work from one of my books with part of a social networking group. The place was perfect – rustic and eclectic – delightfully tasty salads and amazing wraps. The Pineapple Blossom Tea Room in Miami proved to be a perfectly painted canvas for my introduction to a young woman who introduced herself as someone writing a book on finding peace.

Finding peace? Is peace missing? Did someone take peace? Hello!!! Where is peace? I was intrigued by the notion that there was a quest to find peace afoot. I became even more intrigued when I found myself thinking about whether or not I managed or lived my life from a perspective of peace. I wondered if the balance, tranquility even in perplexity, calmness in the storm and overall positive viewpoint that come with peace were evident and prevalent in my life. I decided that the questions were definitely worth some self assessment. I also knew, having done literary-based empowerment workshops, that there are a lot of women who in fact are not living peaceful or authentic lives. They are in fact living lives dictated by various relationships, the decisions of others and the demands of daily life with every one else at the top of the list except them.

Is peace missing? Did someone take Peace? Or have we begun to live lives unaware that it has slipped away from us. Is it possible that peace is lurking in the shadows waiting for us to search for it? Would you recognize peace if it encountered you: at your church, conference, business meeting or networking function?

I believe with every fiber of my being that not only should we live our lives in an overall air of peace; but we should daily grab hold of a little piece of peace and let it embrace our lives. We should daily find enough peace to wipe away the tears of stress, strife and struggle. We should hold on to peace like many of us hold on to our first love letter or first corsage.

Is peace missing in your life? Do not despair - *The Journey to Peace* is a personal and well-thought out map to help you arrive where peace resides. Take this journey determined not to appreciate or consider a concept; but to be immersed in a key component to live life above the chaos.

E. Claudette Freeman, Author
Sheltered Deliverance Pieces.
And Me: A Collection of Life
Arise, Write, Release: The Morning Hour Journal

ONE DAY I'M GONNA CRY

One day I'm gonna cry.

I'm gonna climb to the top of a mountain overlooking a drought-ravaged African village and I'm gonna cry until the crops overcrowd the ground and there will be plenty of food to feed AIDS-infected babies whose only crime was being a virgin.

One day I'm gonna cry.

I'm gonna get down on my knees and cry and release two years or maybe even twelve years of pain.

I'm gonna cry for a little girl who went looking for unconditional love at twenty-one and is still searching for it at thirty-three.

I'm gonna cry until the tears not cried by generations of women who came before me come pouring down my face.

I'm gonna cry for my grandmother who only knew her mother's love, I'm gonna cry for my grandmother who never knew her mother's love. I'm gonna cry for my mother who never knew her father and who only saw her mother when she was standing over her ripping apart her back for imagined crimes.

I'm gonna cry for thirteen year old girls whose fathers call them whores, who in search of love lost what was most precious.

One day I'm gonna cry for all the women whose husbands say I don't want you anymore, whose kids get buried under the rubble of another family disaster.

One day I'm gonna cry for all black women who just get tired of trying and got tired of crying.

One day I'm gonna cry for all the women who fall asleep next to their husbands and still pray to help them overcome loneliness.

One day I'm gonna cry and the words I was told I couldn't say are gonna come pouring down my face.

One day I'm gonna cry and nobody is gonna tell me that I don't even have the right to cry.

One day I'm gonna cry and people who belong together are gonna find each other because my tears cleared the dusty path.

One day I'm gonna cry and husbands are gonna say I'm sorry to their wives for getting angry that she said goodnight in the wrong tone of voice.

One day I'm gonna cry and broken families are going to reconcile and little children won't be afraid to say hello to their daddies and husbands will hug their wives and mothers will hug their children.

One day I'm gonna cry and doors will open that had been closed, broken hearts will be mended and empty spaces will be filled with love.

One day I'm gonna cry and nobody will be around to care and I'm gonna drown in my own tears.

One day I'm gonna cry and pain will go away, cancer will be cured and prayers will be answered.

People will say I love you again,

Husbands will renew their love to their wives and wives will only be with their husbands.

One day I'm gonna cry

Without permission, without excuse, without apologies.

One day I'm gonna cry

just because I want to cry.

Original Poem by
Carol L. Watson

Please pray with me:

Lord, In the name of Jesus, we come before You asking a special blessing for the writer and reader of this book. May this book be the light that guides these wonderful people as they make this journey towards peace. Lord we ask that You speak to us on every page of this book and allow us to recognize Your voice when we hear it. Lord draw us closer to You and closer to Your purpose for our lives. In Jesus' name we submit this prayer.

Amen.

THE PURPOSE OF MY JOURNEY...

Taking inventory of my life was not something I made a conscious decision to do. I found myself in a situation where I had to reevaluate the last few years of my life. I had to figure out how I found myself in a position where I was miserable and losing sleep at night. Peace of mind was coming to me in small intervals and that was not occurring often enough. I was unhappy and many times I found myself suffering from depression. I had artificial forms of happiness, but artificial happiness; such as shopping, eating, sex and manufactured peace (pretending all is well and right with the world) was short lived and I longed for much more.

I saw people around me that seemed to be happy. Some of these people were single, some were married, some had more income than me and some had less. Additionally some were homeowners, while some were renters. There was something, I discovered that was different about them and it turned out to be a significant difference. They were at peace with themselves. Regardless of their situation, they were living the lives they wanted to live. They were living their lives authentically.

There is a great amount of peace that comes with living the life you choose. When you are living your life "on purpose", doing the things that bring you joy and contentment, you will find happiness and that happiness leads to peace. You have to find your peace; understanding that what you find peaceful may be totally opposite of what brings another person peace. For example, I have one sibling, my younger sister Lisa. We grew up in the same house, with the same parents and we have the same gene pool, yet we are totally different and we both find our peace in different places. Lisa and I have a lot of things in common, we both sincerely like each other, and we love the same types of movies and television shows. We both love the same types of food and we laugh at the same stupid jokes. We agree that our parents can be annoying most of the time but we both love and appreciate them all of the time. Even with everything that we have in common we both find our peace in different settings. I prefer the serenity of a quiet neighborhood; my sister prefers a cramped Manhattan apartment overlooking Penn Station. I could never live in the city she loves, but it makes her happy. She cannot imagine a lifestyle that involves adopting and raising three children. I cannot relate to a life that involves moving to a city where I know practically no one, choosing a career that involves globetrotting or deciding to never get married and never have children. Although I cannot imagine that life, the important thing is; that is the life she chooses to live and by doing so, Lisa is living her life authentically. She makes no apologies for who she is and she has all the accolades that go along with being who you wish to be. Lisa is the perfect example of a person who makes the decision early in life, to live authentically and at peace. Do not get me wrong, Lisa is nuts. She will not pick out a comforter for a bed or a piece of art or a rug without emailing me a picture of it to help her decide. Once, I flew out to where she lived to help her choose furniture and decor for her bistro style dining room (Oh, I guess I should mention that I am nuts too) but when it comes to the important decisions that affect her life, she makes them on her own.

Unlike my little sister, I had a totally different situation. I did not always make decisions based on what would make me happy. I did not always take the bold steps toward peace. Then something very simple happened. I woke up one morning determined to live the rest of my life doing the things I love and living a life that would bring me peace. I made a decision to live peacefully. That was it. I simply made the decision. That is how the journey begins; with a decision.

I took stock of all the things I loved most about my life and chose to focus on that; and at the same time I made an effort to minimize all the things that brought me the most stress. I had a friend at the time that was very negative. Every conversation we had was like therapy for him. Every conversation revolved around him complaining about what was wrong in his life, and I just listened because first of all, my advice was never asked for, and secondly, my opinion would not have changed his attitude. Meanwhile, I was absorbing his bitterness in large doses, and could not figure out why his conversations always depressed me. I realized that relationship was stressful for me and so I ended that friendship. I quickly realized that there were some things in my life that stressed me, but I could do very little about those things. All of us have situations like that. For some of us, the stress in our lives comes from our children. This is the type of situation that we have little control over in the sense that this person will always be your child. For some of us the stress factor could be a parent, or a spouse, student loans and high taxes. My point is this, change what you can change and the peace you encounter will help you deal effectively with the things you cannot change.

There is no formula for happiness, peace or contentment. You have to create the path that suits you best. This book documents the path I chose toward peace. As you go with me on my journey, keep in mind that we are doing this together. Take this journey with me with the understanding that I want you to utilize my experiences to help you avoid some of the mistakes I have made along the way.

I invite you to bring a friend or two along with you. You will need the companionship, and as with any other journey if you get tired, the other person will make a great back up driver to keep you going in the right direction until you are rested enough to take the wheel again.

The great thing about this book is you can start at the beginning and work your way forward or you can start at the end and work your way backwards. Wherever you begin, you will find my sincere thoughts and words. You will discover that I am literally an open book. At the end of each small chapter you will find the words, Take Action. That is where your little assignment comes in. If you utilize the suggestions in that section, you will find that your journey will be easier. All the lessons I've learned to this point, I am sharing with you. I pray that this little book is a blessing to you.

From my heart to yours,

Carol

Journey 1

My Journey Begins...

Peace is a journey of a thousand miles and it must be taken one step at a time.

Lyndon B. Johnson

In June of 1999, I was 29 years old, newly separated, and living on my own for the first time. This is where I believe my journey really began.

My separation was devastating to me and it came (I will admit) unexpectedly. My ex-husband and I had a very turbulent marriage. He suffered from anxiety and depression. The medicine the doctor prescribed did not work well for him and he sought happiness in other places. There was an endless amount of extra – marital affairs and verbal abuse in the relationship and at times the abuse became physical. We had moments of happiness, but they were temporary. When things were great, they were great, but when things were bad, they were extremely ugly and painful. I should have left within the first year, but like a lot of women, I thought I had some magical formula to make the marriage work. I knew the marriage was a disaster, but I did nothing to put an end to the relationship. As cowardly as my ex-husband did it, he was the one who made the decision to leave. In spite of the troubles, his decision to leave crushed me.

I came home one day, June 14, 1999 to be exact, to find my husband and everything he owned gone. There was no letter of explanation, but the wedding band he left on top of the television spoke volumes. I was devastated. For a while I was physically unable to move. I experienced an amazing range of emotions in a few short moments. As I stood in the open doorway, realizing that my world had changed without my permission, I experienced everything from hurt, self-pity, anger and even hate. My world had changed and there was nothing I could do about it. The first person I called was my cousin Sabrina. I am not sure why I called her or what she said when I called; I know that whatever she said to me in those important first moments may have saved my life. What he did by leaving so cowardly was inexcusable and heart breaking. We had been married for 3 years and I felt I deserved better than that cowardly exit. I could not go to work for a few days after this happened. For the first three days I was never alone. My visits consisted of me sitting crying while my visitor sat patiently letting me. My supervisor would leave work early to come and sit with me for hours and would allow others to do the same. When I finally went back to work, no one ever mentioned it again. I did not realize how beneficial those first three days had been for me. It was cleansing in a sense. At the end of the three-day stint, I slept peacefully without being interrupted by bouts of crying. I realized that he not being there was the best thing that could have happened to me. The marriage had been tiring, exhausting and eventful. I needed the break. A couple of years later, my boss asked my opinion about an IPO (Initial Public Offering) that was available for purchase by our company. The stock was selling for $6.66. I advised that we should not buy a stock that was being sold for 666, the sign of the devil. He said, "Come on you don't believe in the devil do you"? I said "of course I do, I was married to him for three years". I had come to realize that my husband leaving, as painful as it was, was a blessing because as much as I hated to admit it at the time, the marriage had been more painful than the separation.

When he left, we were at the end of our lease. I had to find a place I could afford on my own. I found a little place in an area that was going through (unknown to me at the time), the same thing I was about to go through, revitalization.

I was living alone for the first time, and again, it was not by my choice. I had just moved into a little two-bedroom duplex in downtown Hollywood, Florida. Downtown Hollywood sits in a great location in Broward County Florida. I was minutes away from the beach by car, and within walking distance of the main strip, Hollywood Boulevard. Downtown Hollywood was being revived during this time, and this was a place where they had jazz clubs lining the streets, outdoor art festivals, live bands playing in the streets, and plenty of trendy restaurants to choose from. This was truly a great place to live for someone in my situation, but I was unable to see that at first. All I could see was I no longer had the nice apartment in the brand new area of town, and I no longer had the man I was in love with.

I confided to my best friend Sharon that the place I was living in did not feel like home to me. I was surrounded by all of my things, but I felt so far away from home. Sharon told me to light some of my scented candles and relax. She said that when it started to smell like home, it would feel like home. I did just as she advised and before long I was comfortable in that space.

I have always decorated my bedroom to feel like a sanctuary and this place was no different. My bed was adorned with a beautiful comforter and sheets with patterns of flowers, petals and leaves. I had an array of silk floral arrangements and fresh flowers as well as beautiful candles. I had a rug next to my bed that was not only lovely to step unto when I got out of bed, but lovely to look at as well. I had been given a large, beautiful lounge chair with bold pink and white stripes on it and that chair was just right for sitting with a good book. I had beautiful art on the walls as well as a bookshelf which held all of my favorite books. It was a very personal space and it was beautiful. The bathroom was directly across the hall from my bedroom, and one night I ran a bubble bath, lit some candles, and sank into the bathtub. I had the door of my bedroom open, and since I lived alone, I also left the bathroom door open. At a certain point, I opened my eyes, looked out the bathroom door noticing the beauty, appeal and peace of my bedroom. In that moment, I felt so relaxed and at peace, finally. I said out loud, "I love this place." Not only did I feel at home there, I had fallen in love with my space in that moment.

It was not just my space; it was the atmosphere I loved as well. There was nobody there to tell me negative things or make me feel bad about myself. Every item in my home represented the things I loved, because being single and living alone meant not having to compromise my style for the benefit of another. I was on my own for the first time and I was at peace for the first time since I was a little girl.

Being on my own for the first time, also meant paying all my own bills for the first time. It was the first time I was responsible for my own safety and my own comfort.

I had to grow up. I had already made the decision after my separation, not to move back in with my parents, but to step out on my own. Now I had to follow through with that decision.

Things were tough at first. I would frequent different restaurants and stores alone in the evenings. When I was married and out past 8 or 9 at night, I had someone calling to see where I was and when I would be home. Now my cell phone did not ring. No one knew I was not at home, no one noticed that I was not there. Many nights I would be home and that realization made me feel lonely and alone.

It was during one of those nights out that my life turned around. I was at a bookstore in Hollywood browsing the self-help section. I came across a book and the title caught my attention. It was a book by Victoria Moran and it was titled, "Creating a Charmed Life." The book was an easy read and it kept my attention throughout. I was so inspired by this book, that I was prompted to do something I had never done before. I wrote the author. To my surprise, she wrote me back. I learned so many things from that little book, and I made a decision that from that moment on I too would live a charmed existence. I started calling my home the Charmed Cottage. I would say to myself, "what a charmed life I have." Before I knew it, my life was charmed. I decorated my home with things I found to be charming, I went places alone that I found charming and I found a few friends that were not only charming, but were living charmed lives as well. It was an amazing time in my life. For the first time, I was experiencing things around me that had been there all along, but I had been so caught up in grief that I totally missed them. I started to take advantage of the great community I was living in. I walked to Hollywood Boulevard on Friday nights to listen to the bands, have dinner or both. I had coffee and dessert at a sidewalk café and talked with a few interesting people that walked by. If no one else wanted to go out on Tuesday nights to my favorite jazz club and listen to my new favorite band, I would go alone. What a charmed life I had, indeed. When they opened a new Starbucks in Hollywood, I would go there on a Saturday morning, drink my coffee and read the paper. My life had slowed down, I was operating at my own pace and for the first time in a long time, it felt great to be me.

I have a few regrets about that time period, decisions I wish I would have made, things I wish I had done differently, but without a doubt those two years, were some of the best days of my life. When I look back on that time; I smile.

Take Action...

Today, as you begin your journey, find your starting point. Your journey may begin at the beginning of this book, or perhaps the fact that you were already on your journey attracted you to this book. Either way, find your starting place. Surround yourself with things and people that represent who you desire to be. Visualize where you wish the road to take you and stay focused on that. Long before my life became charmed I was saying, "What a charmed life I have." Tell your friends that you have begun your journey, by doing so; the inevitable change in your life will not come as a surprise to them. Keep a journal and keep a record of your journey. As you keep this journal you will discover that you are becoming the author of your own story. Take total control of your story. Be careful to keep a map, and map out your route carefully. Learn from my experience and where you read the mistakes I made on my journey, choose a different route.

While on this journey you will undoubtedly come across someone else who is also on this journey. If they have fallen into a pit, stop long enough to help them out. Let's encourage one another, and by doing so, I believe it will make the journey better for us all.

Be blessed, pray, meditate and be authentic.

Journey 2

Carol Watson,
A Pleasure to Meet You,
My Name Is Peace...

*S*he is beautiful. She eludes many because she is seldom where people search to find her.

I met her one-day ~ it was January 2005. It was a beautiful day, much like today. It was close to the evening hour when I received the invitation to see her. I was taken to the very place where she was.

It was beautiful there~ an indescribable light radiating all around. The light was so brilliant it felt like a strong breeze.

On the day we met, she was wearing a beautiful, long, flowing white dress. It was not the type of dress one would wear out, but certainly the type of dress one would wear at home when expecting unexpected visitors.

It was elegant, but unassuming. Peace was wearing her hair down that day, absent of ornaments.

She was quiet when I arrived. She never said a word to me, but she was thrilled that I found her in that place on that day.

Although neither one of us spoke that day~ there was much knowledge gained from the silence.

I learned from her on that day. She has a natural beauty, the type that does not require enhancement.

I longed to be present with her in that place again.

She is not easy to find, but she is worth the journey. Her presence is so strong that without her there with me, I am unable to sleep.

When she is present in my life she brings happiness, fulfillment, contentment and joy.

When she is absent I experience tremendous loss.

Without her presence in my life, I am not truly happy. I exist without existing; I have to remind myself to breathe.

She is uncomfortable wherever chaos is present, but if invited she will certainly show up there.

When she appears her presence does not go unnoticed. She is elegant and beautiful. She speaks softly~ her words are few, but she speaks volumes.

Her movements mimic the movement of the ocean. The stars above line up to form the notes of the songs she sings as she tucks me in at night. Only the sun rising at the beach in September can compete with her radiance. She rests in the light of the moon.

She is available to all who diligently seek her. She is free spirited and complex. She is powerful yet unassuming, she is strong but elegant.

I am on my journey to find her and I find her at every turn along the way.

Journey 3

A Good Place to Start...

Peace starts within each one of us. When we have inner peace, we can be at peace with those around us. When our community is in a state of peace, it can share peace with neighboring communities, and so on. When we feel love and kindness towards others, it not only makes others feel loved and cared for, but it helps us also to develop inner happiness and peace.

Quoted by the 14th Dalai Lama

hat is peace?

I like to ask this question to people now that I am writing a book about the journey to find peace. It never fails that when I ask the question, people have to think hard about what it means to them and then they have to think about whether or not they have found it. The truth is that I did not think about my own peace until God instructed me that I would be writing a book about it.

I was riding in my car in February 2005 and I heard God speak to me. By this time in my life I was used to hearing His voice, so I was able to recognize the manner in which He spoke when speaking to me. He gave me the title. I questioned Him as to what it was that He was telling me. He told me that was the title of the book I was writing. I of course said that I was not writing a book, because at the time I was neither writing a book or considering writing one. Prior to this project, I had only written some poetry and a few bible studies, so I was a little surprised to hear the voice of God telling me that I was writing a book. As it turned out, I had been living my book and now He wanted it in writing.

Knowing that you are not at peace with yourself, your life... is an important acknowledgment to make before deciding to take this journey. Most people do not realize that they are not living a peaceful existence until someone comes along and writes a book about finding your inner peace.

We tend to know that something is not quite right with our lives but we consider it to be an issue related to stress or its demonic big brothers, anxiety and depression. We need to look at the issues of discontent in our lives as issues of peace; then and only then can we start our journey towards peace.

I spent time thinking about peace and evaluating where I was in my life as it related to being at peace. It was during this time when I realized that peace indeed is a conscious journey that requires daily travel.

Peace eludes many of us because we tend to look for it in the wrong place. We look to find our peace in our relationships with others but the reality is that the peace we seek can only be found within ourselves.

In order to understand peace I tried to research it for myself. It was very important to me that when I was directed to document my journey; that I understand fully this entity that is peace. What I found is that very little is known about the topic and although the dictionaries have definitions for peace, little can be found on how to obtain it.

Peace is described by Merriam – Webster's as a state of tranquility or quiet; Freedom from disquieting or oppressive thoughts or emotions and harmony in personal relationships.

An entry on Wikipedia defines inner peace as a state of mind, body and perhaps soul, a peace within ourselves... asserting that an individual may experience inner peace even in the midst of war.

Take Action...

Today would be a great time to start thinking about peace. What brings YOU peace? I am sure you have spent most of your life trying to please others and make them happy, now is the time to think of yourself. Write down the things you know for sure that bring you peace and also what you believe will bring you peace. At the end of this book I want you to do the same thing. Take note to see how that list may change.

Journey 4

Forgiveness...

Make allowance for each other's faults and forgive anyone who offends you. Remember the Lord forgave you, so you must forgive others.

Colossians 3:13 (The Holy Bible,
New Living Translation)

Each of us have people in our lives that fall into one of two categories; we need to forgive them or they need to forgive us. Forgiveness is very powerful when given and received. Many of us know of at least one person who passed away without us either asking them to forgive us for something, or without us forgiving them.

Often times we allow ego to prevent us from forgiving someone, or we allow our ego to prevent us from asking for forgiveness. The interesting thing about the latter is that the person that we have wronged knows that we wronged them. By going to that person and asking for forgiveness, we are not belittling ourselves, we are humbling ourselves. The act of humbling ourselves puts us in a position where we can be blessed.

The Bible tells us in Colossians 3:13 that we should forgive as we have been forgiven. The truth is that forgiving someone also lets us off the hook. We put too much energy into harboring ill feelings toward another human being. Many illnesses can be caused by the stress involved with harboring bitterness. We need to let go and forgive. In an ideal world, everyone who has ever wronged us will step forward and beg us to forgive them. The reality of the situation is that not everyone is on this journey toward peace, not everyone has arrived where you are. There are those that are still being controlled by ego, so you are going to have to do something that goes against everything you have ever been taught about forgiveness. Like myself, you may have to forgive someone who has not even asked for forgiveness.

When I was thirteen years old someone who worked with my dad molested me. My dad trusted this man so much that he allowed him to pick me up from my high school one day. In fact, on many occasions he left my sister and me alone with him in their office. I liked this man. I was usually very intuitive as a child but I never felt uncomfortable when I was around him.

Then one day while my sister and I were alone at the office with him, he touched me. It was only touching and it was upper body. He lifted my shirt to tickle me and I immediately knew this was not right. What started as tickling my stomach ended with him fondling my breasts. I was afraid and I wanted to run to the bathroom and cry, but I knew I had to protect my little sister. There was no time for me to think about what had just happened to me, and crying, which would have upset my little sister, was not an option. I spent the rest of the afternoon guarding her to make sure the same thing did not happen to her. My mother came to pick us up that day. I remember looking at her when we were in the elevator going to the bottom floor. I still recall how I must have looked at her and I clearly recall how she looked at me. As a mother now, I know that a mother's instinct is unfailing and my mother knew something was wrong. The second we got home I went into my room and started to cry. My mother came into my room, stood in my doorway, and I will never forget what she said. My mother said, "He touched you, didn't he?" When I look back on it, I realize how hard that had to be on my mom. My mother told my father about it. I remember my dad telling me that he asked the man about it and he denied it. I grew up thinking my father believed him and not me. Later, as an adult I realized that we were never at my father's office alone with that man again. I also do not remember their work relationship extending far past that day. This man not only worked with my dad, but he lived behind us for many years; so obviously I did see him a few times after that.

Many years later I walked into my parents' garage and the man was there speaking with my dad. I was an adult by that time, but we were raised to speak to our parents' friends, and we always addressed them as Mr. or Mrs.; however, on this occasion, I did not say a word to him, not even hello. I felt numb. His family had moved many years before and I had not seen him. I felt cold when I saw him and everything I hated about him came rushing back to me in that moment. When I saw him in my parents' garage he was 20 feet away from me, but I could clearly feel his hands on me. Seeing my father having a friendly conversation with the man who had molested his little girl made me sick to my stomach. When I got home later that day, I cried, the same way I had done so many years before. My father never said anything to me about not speaking to him and I never said anything to my dad. A short while later I learned that he had passed away. I always hoped that before he died he would tell me he was sorry for what he had done to me. I always wished that he would admit the truth to my father and ask him for forgiveness for betraying his trust. I always hoped he would beg my mother for forgiveness for what he put her through. He never asked. He took that to his grave and I never got the vindication I thought I needed. I hated him. I hated the fact that he never apologized for his actions. As an adult, I had to realize that he was a very sick and troubled old man. I did not feel bad about him being dead; I never felt that emotion people feel when they find out someone they knew has passed away.

The time did come when I had to forgive him. Although he was already deceased, forgiving him allowed me to move forward. Taking this journey toward peace could not take place without me forgiving him.

Just like I had to forgive, I have had to ask for forgiveness. In my life I have made decisions that not only affected others, but hurt them also. I think all adults should call their parents and apologize for the agony they caused their parents during their teenage years, because surely I am not the only person that lost their mind at twelve years old. Your peace is not based on the other person's willingness to forgive you, it is based on your humbleness and your willingness to admit the wrong-doing and ask for forgiveness.

Take action...

Today, get a sheet of paper and draw a line down the middle. On one side write down a list of people that you need to forgive and on the other side write down a list of those you need to ask for forgiveness. On the top of the list of people you need to forgive, place your own name. I am certain that at some point in your life you have done something that you need to forgive yourself for. Dropping out of high school, not graduating from college, having sex as a teenager, getting pregnant, having an abortion, committing adultery, lying to someone you care about, using illegal drugs, ending a relationship with someone who did not deserve it, ruining your credit, disrespecting your parents, (fill in the blank) _____. Today is the day that you get to forgive yourself. Making mistakes is part of the process. As a matter of fact, it is an important part of this journey. We not only learn from our mistakes, we grow from them.

After you make the list, follow through with the process. When you are finished forgiving and asking for forgiveness, destroy the list. Destroying the list is your way of doing away with these past mistakes and moving forward to your destination.

Journey 5

The Source of Peace (How Well Do You Know Him?)...

It is my belief that God is the source of peace. I know that my inner peace is directly related to my relationship with Him. I spend a lot of time studying my bible because through the process of study and prayer; I get to really know God and understand Him. It is this relationship I have with Him that allows me to know His voice when I hear it. Therefore when I hear something in my spirit that says something like…adopt three kids or write this book, or (and this is my personal favorite) pray for someone I do not really like a whole lot, I never have to question that it is God speaking to me.

My son Travey reminded me of how important it is to really get to know someone and the very personality of that person. One morning as I was getting my kids prepared for school, I noticed that their room had a box filled with garbage in it. They had done some spring-cleaning the day before, and neglected to take the garbage out. I asked Travey to get the garbage ready to go, and we would drive it to the dumpster on the way to school. Travey turned his back while I was still talking so that he could get the box. While he had his back turned I noticed there were dirty clothes on their floor, instead of in the bathroom hamper as they should have been. I told Travey to put the dirty clothes in 'there', pointing to the bathroom hamper. Travey did not see where I was pointing because he still had his back turned. I finished getting ready for work, did my daughters hair for school, loaded the kids and the garbage into the car and drove to the dumpster in our community. As Travey grabbed the box to take it to the trash, I noticed that the dirty clothes were in there.

I asked him how the clothes ended up in the box with the garbage. Having his back to me, he thought I had asked him to put the clothes in the garbage. I had the kids grab the clothes out of the box and Travey got out of the car to go the dumpster. After he closed the car door, I turned around and said to my son John and my daughter Janel; "Travey is crazy." You would have to know me to understand what I did when Travey got back in the car. I tried to start trouble. My boys are only 6 months apart in age and are very close. They have everything in common and as a general rule, they get along quite well (for siblings). When Travey got back in the car I immediately said; "Travey, John called you crazy." John never got a chance to say anything to defend this lie because almost immediately Travey responded. Travey said, "I know John and I know he did not say that." I, of course, tried to argue my point. Then Travey went on to say, "I know John and he did not say that, you did." I said, "Travey, I am your mommy and you know me too." He said, "I do know you, and that is how I know you said it."

The entire carload of us burst into laughter. Travey had caught me in my mischief and called me on it. John never had to defend himself because Travey knows us so well that he knows who would say what.

This is how it should be between God and us. We should never have to rely solely on what others tell us about God, we need to come to understand Him for ourselves. We need to develop a relationship with God, and through that relationship with Him we gain a sort of peace that cannot be manufactured.

Take Action...

Today, if you have not already done so, get to know God on a very personal level. There is no other relationship more beneficial to our well being then a relationship with Him.

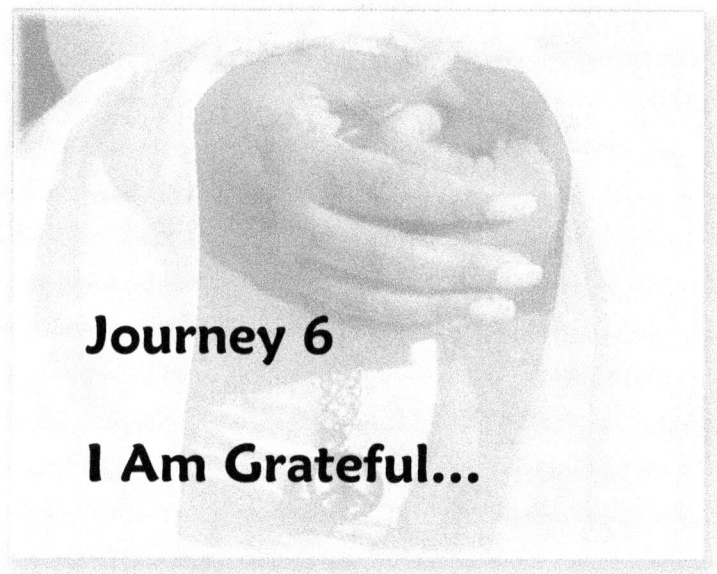

Journey 6

I Am Grateful...

In the same year that this journey began for me, I was sitting in my doctor's office waiting to be seen. At the time I was working as an assistant for a successful Stock Broker at a well-respected firm. The stock market was closed for the Fourth of July holiday and I tried to utilize my days off for my non-emergency appointments. The staff had the television on in the waiting room and a very popular talk show was on. On the show was a self-help author talking about the importance of keeping a journal and more importantly, the significance of keeping a gratitude journal. Every day she proposed that you should write down things you are grateful for. I honestly do not recall what the author said was significant about it, but here is what I learned after starting to keep my own gratitude journal.

Keeping this journal forced me to focus on the positive things that were happening in and around me. I began to notice everything. I would write things in my journal that read similar to this... I am grateful for the cup of coffee I had today. Now understand this, being grateful for the cup of coffee may have had very little to do with the coffee itself. I was probably grateful for the conversation I had that day with the Barista that prepared the coffee for me, or perhaps I was grateful that while I was at the coffee shop, an interesting person came in, or some other similar experience. My point is that my gratitude journal did not have to go into details; it could be as vague as I wanted it to be.

This special little journal helped me to maintain an attitude of gratefulness, because every day I had to write what I was grateful for. I wanted everyone to feel the same amount of contentment I felt. I went to the dollar store and purchased a bunch of blank journal–style books. On the inside cover, I wrote the person's name and below their name I wrote the concept of the gratitude journal. I also gave a little history about it, told them how it had helped me. Then I encouraged them to utilize the journal for that purpose.

I learned a lot from keeping a gratitude journal. For instance, I have always been afraid of thunderstorms, and living in Florida intensifies that fear for me. I would not hesitate to say what a nasty day it was on those days when the rain seemed relentless. Keeping a gratitude journal helped me to appreciate that a rainy day was not a nasty day; it was simply a wet day. That one simple change in thought made such a big difference in my approach and attitude. Instead of sitting trapped in the house, day in and day out, hoping that the rain would stop, I began to appreciate the beauty in storm. Storms stir things up in the atmosphere, and a really great storm does wonders for a dirty sidewalk in desperate need of a good hosing off. Keeping a gratitude journal has also helped me to appreciate my children a little more. I was often aggravated by the strong personalities my children had. What I came to appreciate (while practicing gratitude) is that a strong-willed child becomes an independent adult; even when they face challenges along the way. After all, one of the most important goals of parenting is to raise a child who will become a responsible adult.

Living gratefully means looking for the positives in your everyday life.

Take Action...

Today, go out and purchase a journal that you can utilize as a gratitude journal. Beginners should set a minimum number of daily entries. Make an effort to put at least ten entries into your journal every day. Having a daily assignment to look for positive things to be grateful for will change your outlook on life. A positive attitude is a must have for this journey. As we pursue the God of peace, it is important that we maintain an attitude of gratitude.

Encourage your friends to keep a gratitude journal. Purchase scented candles and tons of inexpensive, yet pretty journals and give them as gifts. You are not just giving the people you care about cheap candles and blank books; you are giving them the tools they need to experience peace also.

Today I am grateful for everyone who made a decision to share in my journey. May you not only find the peace you are searching for, but encourage others as well.

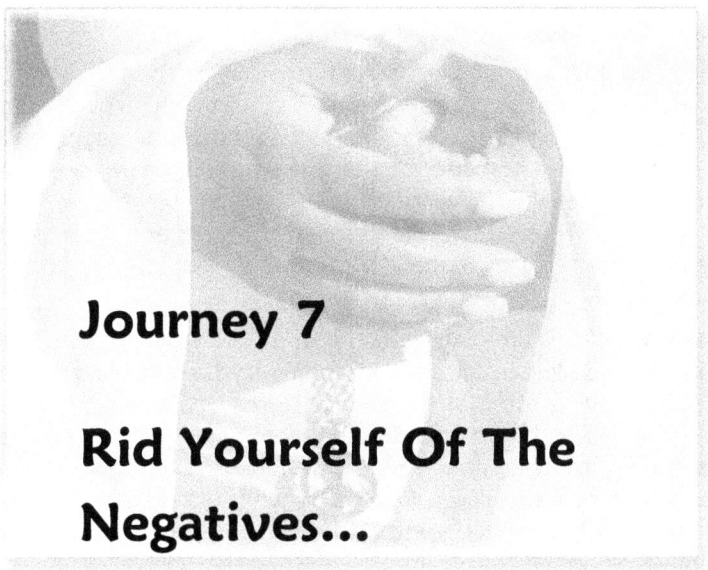

Journey 7

Rid Yourself Of The Negatives...

Every day we are exposed to an abundant amount of junk. In addition to what we allow in through gossip, news, talk radio, and television, we are also exposed to things we have no control over. While riding in my car, I like to listen to inspirational music and soft vocalists like Norah Jones, Corinne Bailey Rae and similar artists. Many times as I am listening and enjoying the soft melodic themes, some person rides up next to me listening to music that I do not necessarily enjoy. This individual may have their music at a volume where everyone around them is forced to listen to the same thing. My favorite unwelcome intrusion is public cell phone use. I have a thing about talking on my cell phone in public. When I am grocery shopping or walking through the mall, I do not like to have conversations on my cell phone. By talking publicly, I am inviting strangers into my very personal conversations. Unfortunately, on a daily basis we are exposed to other people's personal conversations. The next time you are out and someone is talking on his or her cell phone, pay attention to what the conversation is like. More than likely, you are listening to one side of a conversation filled with gossip. I will usually answer my phone when I am out, if only to say I will call back when I get out of the store. If it is a significant other or your kids, it's always a smart thing to answer, make sure it's not an emergency and then let them know you will call back.

The other source of unwelcome information (for me) is television news. I respect news anchors and reporters for what they do, but I do not like the repetitiveness of newscasts. I prefer to get my news from a printed newspaper or the Internet. It's smart to stay informed, but television news exposes us to things we may be trying to avoid. I shy away from entertainment news and news about war, and by reading the news I determine what stories I wish to take in.

I have a difficult time falling asleep in a totally quiet room. Like most people I like to fall asleep listening to the radio or TV. I remember having some of the weirdest dreams after falling asleep with the TV on. I have often found that my dreams were based on a show on my television while I was asleep. The same ears that allow us to hear the alarm clock go off while we are asleep, allows us to hear other things going on around us and not all of those things are positive.

Not all our negative intake comes from music or television. Negative people are probably the biggest area of concern. I am very much for loyalty in friendships and I understand the importance of having friends, but as you begin this journey, it is important to take inventory of your friends.

There are some relationships we will not be able to do anything about. Being married to a negative person is not grounds for divorce, and understand that divorce is very painful and can have spiritual ramifications to the person who requests a divorce for the wrong reasons. If the basis of their negativity is abuse and /or adultery, then of course a permanent separation is a legitimate course of action. Also, negative family members are another relationship we can do very little about. We do have the option to limit the contact we have with them.

I do not recommend making a list of the culprits, calling them up and then cutting them down at their knees. Make a list of your family and friends that you consider to be negative influences in your life. Call them up one by one and inform them about the journey you are on. They do not have to understand your decision they just need to listen and respect your decision to make this lifestyle change. Give them an opportunity to make the changes needed to continue playing an active role in your life. Do not give ultimatums such as, "if you do not change, we will not be hanging out anymore." In reality, you cannot expect someone to change for the benefit of your peace, but if this person wishes to remain a part of your inner circle, they need to monitor their attitude around you.

My older cousin Freeman Jr. is known more for his honesty than his tactfulness. I called his cell phone at the start of a new year and the greeting on his phone shocked me and entertained me at the same time. This is what his message said; "You have reached Freeman. I am making some changes in my life right now. Please leave a message for me, if I do not call you back then you are one of the changes I made."

I had never heard such a message. It was as honest as he usually is, so it should not have been a surprise, but who says such things? Well thankfully, he called me right back, so that was good thing. His message was a clear indication to every caller that he was removing the negatives.

I had a friend who I absolutely loved. In my opinion she suffers from an undiagnosed form of depression that makes her experience severe mood swings. She has extreme highs and lows, and she has no sense of responsibility when it came to her mood. It always seemed to be someone else to blame for her negative mood, words and behavior. The people who use to hang around her never gave valid reasons for changing their relationship status with her, because they felt it was pointless. Instead of talking to her, they just ended the relationship. There were days when I felt the life drain out of me just from being exposed to her attitude. I need you to fully understand that I adored this woman; however, having a friendship with her was pleasant at times and exhausting the rest of the time. I had to have the conversation with her when it became obvious that in order to continue on this journey she would either have to change her approach to our friendship or I would have to endure the process of ending the relationship.

Once we have the conversation, we need to give the other person the opportunity to adjust. Our decision to change our destination came after much thought and preparation. We have had time to make adjustments. In order to be fair, we have to give them time also. If it becomes obvious that this person is not going to adjust, we will have to make the decision to change the status of that relationship. There have been times when I have endured the pain of a negative relationship just to avoid the pain involved in ending the relationship. As crazy as that sounds, we all do it. Take inventory of your past relationships. Remember that man or woman that ended your relationship and you spent days feeling silly because you were thinking, "how dare _____ leave me, I was the one who should have left his/her silly acting self."

There does come a point in our lives when we need to make the decision to walk away. Women are built from very strong fabric and we have the ability to endure a lot. Because of this, we tend to stick it out, make adjustments when needed, and then stick it out some more. Only when we feel we have tried everything over and over again without success, do we then make the decision to walk away. We feel like failures because we always believe we should have tried one more time. The truth is that no matter how many more times we would have tried, we would have not been successful.

In most cases, the more work you put into something, the more you contribute, the more you hang in there, the more successful you will be. Toxic relationships are not one of those situations. Toxic relationships are not limited to intimate relationships, this can also occur between friends and family members. Any relationship you have that causes you pain, physically, mentally or emotionally can be classified as toxic. It does not matter how hard you try, it will never be enough for the other person.

Pardon me for a moment; I feel the need to interject something important. I do not want to make light of your individual situation. I know from experience how difficult it is to walk away from a toxic relationship. We feel that our presence in this person's life will somehow save them from themselves. I understand, believe me. Some of us are in relationships we have already decided to leave; we are just waiting for the right moment, or hoping that the person may change indeed. You need to make the decision for yourself and not base it on someone else's opinion, experience or otherwise. The only way I would firmly state to you to leave now is if your relationship is abusive. We have a responsibility to keep ourselves safe and protected. In 1999, when I was forced into a situation where I found myself alone, I thought I could not manage. Thank God, I was wrong. If I was able to do it, I feel strongly that you can as well.

Take Action...

Today, take inventory of all your relationships. Those relationships that leave you feeling drained, make a note to speak with that person about your journey, give them time to adjust, but if they do not make the necessary efforts to maintain the friendship, cordially and respectfully bow out. Surround yourself with positives; you will need this for your journey. Be responsible for what you take in. Understand that you cannot control everything that you take in, but control what you can, filter what you can and understand that what you cannot control or filter, is just part of your growth on the journey. If you find yourself single right now, value whatever time you have alone, knowing that soon that space will be filled with someone who wants to go along on your journey. Had I known in 1999, that I would have ended up adopting three beautiful children a few years later, I would have taken better advantage of that time alone.

I found a statement in a magazine that said "A Peaceful Mind." I taped that statement on my dashboard and whenever I get into my car, I am reminded that my goal is a peaceful mind. As you start your journey, or continue your journey, place these little "road maps" around to remind you of your destination.

Let's take this moment to pray together:

Lord, we come before You at this time asking for Your guidance in dealing with toxic relationships. We realize how important peace is to our relationship with You since You are the God of peace. Right now we ask that as we make the decision to leave toxic relationships that You be with us. We understand that we will feel lonely at times without this person in our lives, but we know You will never leave us alone. We trust that You will be with us on this journey as our Guiding Light and we thank You in advance.

In Jesus' name we submit this prayer.

Amen.

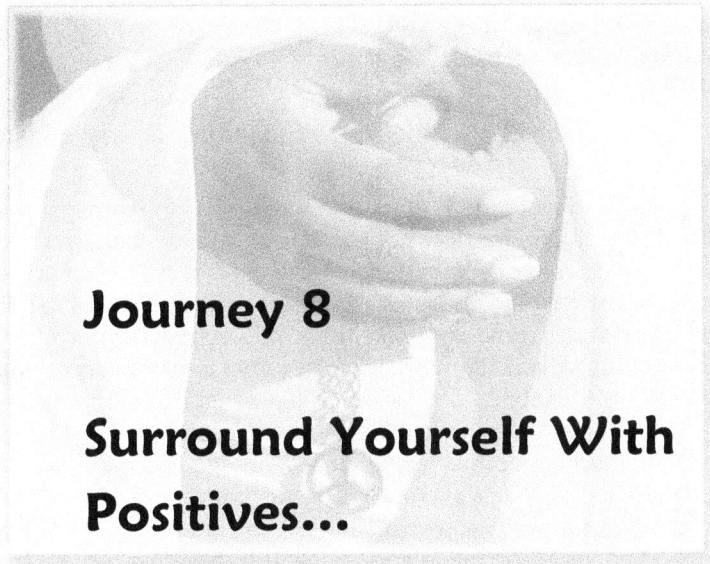

Journey 8

Surround Yourself With Positives...

Once you rid yourself of negatives, make sure to surround yourself with positive things, words and people. I have this theory that we are affected by what goes on around us whether it be positive or negative. We will find more peace along the way if we are surrounded by positives.

I have had my share of negatives but I have been fortunate enough to have an abundance of positives. I have awesome children, a sister that is amazing, parents that love me in spite of myself, my forever friend Carlos (who I can always count on for some good humor), a best friend Sharon that has put up with me for over 20 years, despite the fact that she has to call me on her birthday every year to remind me to tell her happy birthday, yet she never forgets mine.

Sharon is my friend that I can call at eight in the morning and ask her to relax my hair, and she shows up within the hour. Or I can call her in the middle of the night crying and she holds the phone until I am able to put words together.

Then of course there is Michelle. Michelle has been a saving grace for me on too many occasions to mention. She brings humor, dependability and sanity to me at times when I seem to carry the weight of my world on my shoulder.

It is because of relationships like this that I feel empowered to continue moving forward even when I feel like I have hit a brick wall, or when I feel like a brick wall has crashed down on me.

I find that as I make this journey to find peace, the more I surround myself with positives, the easier it is to find the peace I am searching for.

My grandmother Leasie is at an age where she is feeling nervous about living alone. She does not feel as healthy as she did years ago, but this is normal for someone in their late 80's. A lot of families would be collecting brochures of nursing homes, but my family fights for her to come live with them. Everybody wants her to come live with them. If my grandmother goes to her mailbox without calling someone, phone calls get generated from family member after another trying to find out who has whisked her away. My grandmother became very ill some years ago and we were told that she had to have a surgery she might not recover from. We were at that hospital taking over the waiting area and her hospital room. My uncle Rob made arrangements to have her moved to a different hospital than the one she was first admitted to, ensuring that his mother- in- law would get the appropriate care. Even in her weakened state she was aware that we were all surrounding her, loving her. I strongly believe that my grandmother survived a very difficult time in her life because she was surrounded by positives.

What you surround yourself with can make a difference between peace and despair, life or death. There are so many things that we are exposed to on a regular basis that we have little control over. This is the reason we have to do everything we can to surround ourselves with as many positives as possible. Take precautions in what you allow into your world. Not everyone we meet should be invited on our journey. Some people we meet are prime candidates to take this journey with us. Some people we meet are the main reason why we need to make this journey.

My writing consultant/publisher Claudette, recently put together a Detoxification Kit. The purpose of this kit is to help people examine their lives and decide who in their lives is a positive and who is a negative. The positives get a note card in the mail or a phone call saying something like "hey, you're great, I am glad you are in my life." The negatives get a note that amounts to something like, "see ya." It sounds kind of cruel, but in the end, it is all about creating a positive environment for you.

Take Action...

Today, make the decision to surround yourself with positive things and positive people. Your journey to peace will be fueled by the outcome.

Journey 9

Faith on Your Journey...

Lord, I really need your help in dealing with this situation regarding my job. Lord you know I have a difficult time dealing with my boss but I really need this job. Lord I am totally leaning and depending on You.
Amen.

"While God is working on this situation for me, I am going to figure out what I can do, just in case the situation gets worse. Maybe I should call_____, and get her opinion on what I should do about this, oh and maybe I can call _____ to see if he has heard of any job openings at his company, just in case."

Does that little scenario sound familiar? Regrettably, I have gone through this scene numerous times. I pray and ask God to help me with one situation or another and then before I can get off my knees good, I am making back up plans. Having a backup plan is smart, but having a backup plan to something you've already asked God to take care of, shows a lack of faith.

I have lost many nights sleep, worrying over a situation that I have already prayed about. I come up with a few "just in cases", in case

God does not follow through. When the situation gets handled, I thank God and praise Him as if I've trusted Him all along.

I always end up feeling like a fraud. I talk faith, I write about it and at the same time I often lack it. The truth is, a lack in faith causes me, and a lot of other women many sleepless nights; and sleepless nights do not promote peace. Faith in God is an essential element of this journey towards peace.

We have been taught to be self sufficient, which means relying on ourselves when all others fail, but this self-reliance is unnecessary when we understand that we should lean completely on God. I know that the practice of this faith is easier taught than practiced, but we must make every effort to rely on the God we pray to, or stop praying. Whenever someone tells me, "If you pray why worry, if you worry why pray", I get very annoyed. People only say that to someone when they themselves are not going through anything at the moment. The truth is, that regardless of how annoying that catchy little phrase is, it is also very true. We pray to God out of faith, and we worry due to a lack of faith. These two frames of mind clash at every turn. We must learn to trust God to do what He says He will do.

I make excuses for not trusting God to come through for me. I know that I do not always make the decisions He would want me to make, and I know many times I have stepped outside of His will, so I usually expect God not to show up for me. It is important to remember though, that God is our Father. As parents, we have time and time again come to the rescue of our wayward child; just like our parents rescued us even during those times we disappointed them. If not you, then surely you know of the mother who has mortgaged her home to get her child out of jail for a crime he or she certainly did commit. Or how about the dad who empties his bank account to rescue his son from another financial disaster, or holds the hand of his thirteen year old daughter while she goes through a procedure to get rid of an accidental pregnancy, or the mom who holds her daughters hand while she gives birth at fifteen.

Parents forgive and love their children anyway. God is no different. He loves us despite the many messes we find ourselves in, and time after time, He shows up for us.

God is always going to do what God says He will do. It is our guilt that prevents us from trusting. We know we don't deserve this type of devotion, so we second-guess God.

Whatever has happened in your life that caused your lack of faith or made you believe that God is no longer in your corner, ask God to forgive you. Trust me, He will.

Take Action...

Today, take inventory of the times you asked God for help with something and then tried to do it on your own. How did things work out? Now think about all the times you asked God to help you and He did. If you are anything like me you will find that in each situation God kept His word. The difference is, when you asked and worried you had no peace during the process. When you asked and waited, you were at peace knowing God was doing His thing.

Journey 10

Visualize The Journey...

It is very important to tell people who we are. My name is Mary and I am the president of a large corporation, or my name is Paul and I am a spoken word artist. Whoever you are, feel free to let others know. During the course of writing this book people asked me the question, "what do you do for a living?" After I give them the rundown of whatever I do to support myself, I throw in that I am also writing a book. They usually assume that I am writing a fictional novel; I correct them and tell them I am writing a guidebook to finding inner peace.

Now, you know what comes next don't you? Of course you do. They feel that because I am writing a book on finding peace that I have "arrived" at peace. Well let me inform you as I have informed the others. "I am on this journey the same way you are." Peace is something that we hope to find in our eternal resting place. Until then, it is the journey toward peace that brings us the peace we are seeking. Every day that we are on this journey we are making the types of decisions that bring us peace.

I have found that while I am on this journey, being able to visualize the journey is essential.

I wrote previously about the road maps we need on this journey. I have this framed picture that hangs in my master bathroom. I have had this piece of art for over three years. The picture hung in a place in my old bathroom that made it hard to miss whenever I went to the bathroom. If we average how many times a person visits the bathroom in their home and then multiply it by 365 days for 3 years, you can pretty much figure how often I have been confronted with this picture. The picture depicts a beautiful woman standing on her back porch looking out over a lake. She looks to be at peace, and even without realizing it I was visualizing that view for myself. When I moved into my new home, the master bath was the last thing I organized. I hung the picture up and after hanging the picture I realized that the picture I was looking at was my new back yard. One of the things that attracted me to this house was the fact that the master bedroom was on a separate floor from the other bedrooms (those of you who have kids understand), and the fact that the house was on a lake. I did not make a conscious effort to get the view that was in the picture, but when you visualize something for yourself day in and day out, more than likely you will get it. It is very important that we surround ourselves with visuals of things that we want for ourselves. I am not speaking purely of material things; I am speaking spiritually as well.

When I was a little girl, there was a very popular sitcom depicting a poor black family who never could manage to keep their heads above water. Everyone I knew loved that show. Something about the show never appealed to me. As I got older I realized what it was that kept me from watching the show. Yes the show was funny and yes the family loved each other, even when the siblings were fighting amongst themselves, they loved each other. However, no matter what they did, at the end of the show all efforts toward success had failed and they were right back where they started. Even as a young child I knew there was something disturbing about people who looked like me on television, depicting failure.

I wrote before about the phrase "A Peaceful Mind" that I cut out of a magazine and posted on my dash. Peace is what I visualize for myself and as we make this journey together I advise that you also post things in areas that you frequent such as your bathroom mirror, your refrigerator, or the dash in your car that will remind you of your destination. These little road maps or road markers are essential for this journey toward peace.

Keep a journal of your journey. In your journal keep track of your progress and write your goals as well. Read and reread those goals and watch how easily you will accomplish them.

Take Action...

Today, search for visuals to post around your space. If you cannot find phrases about peace in magazines, create your own on your computer, or visit a spiritual bookstore and purchase those cute little cards with the inspirational phrases on them. Surround yourself with visuals that depict positives. What you visualize you will accomplish, so make it count.

Journey 11

Find Your Peaceful Place...

While on this journey it is important that we have a place we can go that gives us peace. For some people that peaceful place might be a place of worship. Others find their peace in different places and one individual could have several peaceful places. For me my place of peace varies depending on what I need that particular day.

There are days when I can only find it while sitting on the floor in the aisle at the bookstore reading a magazine. Other days, I find the most peace at my local coffee shop. When I am going through difficult times, I can only find the peaceful moment I am searching for at the beach watching the sunrise or at night watching the waves under a beautiful starry night. My brother Frantz built a sanctuary of peace in his back yard.

The longer you are on the journey toward peace, the easier it is to be at peace wherever you are. However, having a peaceful place is important at any stage of your journey. Daily we need to pursue peace, and daily we may need to be reminded of our journey. Having a place to go that brings you peace is a good way to stay focused on the journey.

A few years ago Lisa and I, along with our parents, went on a seven-day Alaskan cruise. I fell in love with Alaska and my love affair with that beautiful land has endured since that time. I recall standing on the deck of the ship with several strangers starring across the water at spectacular blue glaciers. The water was so still and calm that it appeared that you could walk across the top of the water to the other side. It was very cold on the deck even though it was the middle of June. Everyone on the deck was dressed in warm clothing and wrapped in blankets provided by the cruise line. We were all standing there quietly looking in amazement at the beautiful sight before us. There are no words to describe the beauty and majesty I witnessed. What appeared before me could only be described as nature at its best. As I stood there, I felt closer to God than I had ever felt before. After experiencing Alaska while hiking, whale watching and admiring glaciers, I fell in love with the beauty of God's creation. It was during that trip to Alaska that I realized how much I truly loved nature.

There is never a time I have not felt peaceful while observing the wonder of creation. During moments of unrest I am certain to find peace in a natural environment. Finding your place of peace while on this journey is essential. Find a place that you love whether or not it is an indoor sanctuary or a place outdoors observing the wonders of creation.

Take Action...

Today, think about a place where you have been most at peace. Is it indoors or outdoors? Take a moment today to visit that place. If that peaceful place was discovered while vacationing, find another place closer to home, and visit there today. Embrace the solitude you find while there.

Journey 12

Be Authentically You...

Many of us share a similar life story. As children we learned that pleasing our parents kept them happy with us. We dressed in the clothes they bought us to wear, we behaved (for the most part) the way they told us to behave, we ate the foods they prepared, and we worshiped whatever form of god they worshipped. We spent the early years of our lives mimicking our parents.

We grew up, but we still found ourselves worshipping in the church we grew up in, yet we were not being adequately filled. We still behaved in the manner that pleased our parents, always careful not to disappoint them. We are still living our lives based on our parent's desires but we cannot quite put our finger on why we are unhappy.

I have come into contact with a lot of people on my journey and not all are living their lives authentically. It is my belief (and research proves) that many forms of depression are caused by chemical imbalances in the body; but I also believe there are many who are depressed because they are not living the life they desire to live.

In an ideal world we would all live the way we choose. We would marry whom we want to and not the person our mom picked out. We would join the military and fight for our country, even though our mom promised to disown us if we chose a career path that caused her to lose sleep at night. We would have a same sex partner instead of being afraid to come out to our family and friends. We would go to the college of our choice and not the one that we were forced to go to because it happened to be our parent's alma mater. We would live our own lives. If we wanted to cover our bodies in tattoos or piercings and say the hell with Hepatitis A thru Z, again, our choice. Instead we choose to live the life that was mapped out for us from the very beginning. If we are fortunate, we realize that a change in lifestyle is necessary for our happiness. If we are less fortunate, we stand at what could be the end of our life, look back and realize we never made the decisions we should have made to be happy.

We do not live in an ideal world, so we do have legitimate concerns about our families passing judgment, condemning us or expressing their disappointment in our choices. The bottom line however is that no one has the power to bring us happiness and peace except God and ourselves. Living according to the standards of our families is more about pleasing them and making them happy, than it is about our own happiness.

Whenever we choose to live the opposite of who we are, it does not affect us solely. We should be conscious of how our change in thoughts and lifestyle will affect others. That should not stop us however from making the changes to be authentic.

When a well-known politician decided (after he was already married) to live an alternative lifestyle, he was choosing to live his life authentically. His decision was discussed and dissected throughout many media outlets and destroyed his family in the process. The choice to live authentically can come at a cost, if you have been living a lie thus far.

Living authentically has different meanings to different people. What authenticates one person may not be the same for another. My sister Lisa decided some years ago that she never wants to get married or have children of her own. She is perfectly content being in a committed relationship with a man without marriage. This type of relationship is authentic for her. On the flip side of the coin is a friend who absolutely believes she will not find true happiness unless she gets married and has a child. Although I have expressed to her how difficult marriage can be and how she might want to enjoy the life she has right now, she is convinced that she should be married and therefore that is authentic for her.

Take Action...

Today, take inventory of your life. Have you been living your life authentically? Or have you been living a lie? Make the decision to live your life authentically, but make the transition with the knowledge that others will be affected by your choice. If you are fortunate, you have lived your life authentically, and any minor changes needed will have little effect on your loved ones. If this is not your situation, make wise decisions. Seek the counsel of a minister or another professional to help you with the transition.

Let's pray:

Lord God, we realize that we have gotten to a point in our lives where we have to make the choice to be authentic in order to be at peace with ourselves. We have been very careful to please others and now we need to make a choice to please ourselves. We are not choosing to be selfish or unfair, we are simply choosing to be at peace. We know that You are not a God of confusion and that You are the God of peace, so we ask that You give us Your guidance.

In Jesus' name we submit this prayer.

Amen.

Journey 13

Detours...

I heard some really good advice about dieting and weight loss, and I want to share it with you. While dieting, if you fall off the wagon by adding a few glazed doughnuts to your dinner don't say, "the hell with the diet," and spend your vacation days at the all-you-can-eat buffet. The next day, wake up and get back on the wagon.

That advice works for this journey as well. There may be days when you are not behaving like a woman who is living a life of peace. Someone in traffic cuts you off and blows you off in the process, or an employee makes you blow your stack. You may have taken a vow to clean up your dirty language and someone causes you to use words you thought you had forgotten.

When you come to your senses and calm down, you will undoubtedly feel regret and remorse for your actions. Your first thought may be that you failed on this journey; therefore you may as well give up. I have been there more times than I care to acknowledge, but here is what I've done and this is what I suggest you do as well. Take a moment to reflect on your actions, forgive yourself, ask God to forgive you and continue your journey. If the victim of your foul language was within an earshot, you might want to give them a call as well and apologize.

Setbacks and delays are meant to be temporary. We are not meant to sit on the side of the road permanently. We get discouraged and disappointed in ourselves because we thought we overcame negative behavior. This attitude has never brought us peace, and this situation is no different.

Some of these detours are put in place to make sure we have not fallen asleep while we are driving. They keep us sharp. They keep us awake. They remind us that we need to continue on the journey; because surely we have not arrived.

I have had setbacks and delays while on my journey, and each time I beat myself up over it because I know how I should be handling the situation. So many times I have lost my cool when dealing with situations involving my relationships. I can be very easy going when dealing with my mate. Many times if something ridiculous is said to me I can shrug it off and move on. Then there are those days (usually at the beginning of the month) when one wrong word will cause me to blow my stack. I can say some cruel things when I feel like I have been wronged or mistreated. The more I mature, the easier it is to quickly realize my faults, and I ask for forgiveness rather quickly. It's difficult, but each time we get back on the right track, it gets easier.

Every day we have an opportunity to move forward. Each day brings its' own challenges and rewards. When we feel that we are headed in the wrong direction, we should pick up the phone and call a friend who supports us on our journey. We should not be afraid to ask a friend for prayer or words of wisdom. No matter how you feel, it's hard to stay angry after communicating and praying about the matter.

There have been days when I was too embarrassed to call anyone and talk about what I was going through. On days like that I have found that music (usually inspirational) helps me regain my strength for my journey.

Take Action...

Today, if you have not done so already, invite a friend to go with you on this journey. When you get detoured, they will be there to encourage you. Read your Bible and allow the Word of God to minister to your spirit. Pray and ask God to give you the tools you need to get back on track. If you are not a Bible reader reread pages in your gratitude journal, they will remind you of how blessed you are.

Be encouraged.

Let's pray:

Lord, we come before You at this time and ask that You forgive us for that moment when our words did not represent You. We ask that You give us the tools we need to get back on track. When we search Your Word, we ask that You speak to us through those words. We ask that You direct us to the friend that will best accompany us on this journey, and that we may be continually encouraged.

In Jesus' name, we submit this prayer.

Amen.

Journey 14

Dance to Your Own Rhythm...

I have always been attracted to books, greeting cards, articles or anything that says something like: move to your own beat, or dance like no one is watching. There is something so free about moving to the beat of your own drum. I wrote a poem a few years ago that talks about that very thing.

11/25/03

> I have a song within my spirit.
>
> At times I dance to its rhythm.
>
> The words flow through me with an easy pace. Sometimes I laugh when I hear the lyrics,
>
> sometimes I cry. Sometimes I laugh so hard that I cry.
>
> I can feel the rhythm.
>
> Can you hear what I hear?
>
> Sometimes it's an easy, mellow, smooth type of beat,

Sometimes it moves so fast it makes my heart race.

Some days it's like listening to jazz in the park

early on a Sunday morning,

Some days it's the hip-hop that awakens the downtown Hollywood streets on a Friday night.

Some days I feel like singing!

Some days I just want to hum.

The music feeds my spirit and it speaks to me, speaks thru me.

Nothing else touches me like my own rhythm.

Do you hear what I hear?

I love this poem and not just because I wrote it. There is something so adolescent about moving to your own rhythm. Moms you can relate to this. I laugh when I hear my children singing some crazy song they just made up in their heads. I also get a kick out of seeing my kids dancing. It looks like they are dancing to a different song than the one I am listening too. My little ones know the key to peace and happiness. They are dancing to their own rhythm.

Find your rhythm. You will not find the notes in a book and you cannot be taught the rhythm. Everyone has a unique rhythm.

I met a girl a while back and she paid me a very nice compliment. I am not sure how she meant it, but it really did not matter; I took it the way I wanted to. She told me that I came across as a free spirit to her. Growing up, and perhaps as an adult also, whenever I pictured a free spirit, I pictured a hippy, driving a beetle painted to look tie-dyed, with the peace symbol airbrushed all over it. This free spirited hippie was driving this old beetle to Woodstock reunion concerts, listening to music from the seventies and getting high. However, when she called me a free spirit, I took it totally as a compliment. I had just begun my journey and I really took that to mean that something in my personality represented that peace you get when you do not have a care in the world.

I embraced the compliment and allowed it to fuel my journey. Let the song in your spirit be fuel for your journey. Embrace every opportunity to dance to your own rhythm, and of course, dance like no one is watching.

Take Action...

Today, turn on the radio, turn it up very loud, and dance like no one is watching.

Journey 15

Be Silly, Just For the Heck of It...

I love my sister Lisa. I love a lot of things about her, but one of my favorite things about Lisa is her ability to just be silly. Not only is she silly, I get silly too, especially when I am talking with her. We have laughed at ourselves numerous times over the years, but a particular example comes to mind.

When my maternal grandfather passed away, Lisa came to town to be with my mom and to attend the memorial celebration for my grandfather. Shortly before she came to town, my mother announced to me that some relatives were driving down to be with us, and they would be staying at my house. I found out the day they were coming how many people would be staying at my house and the number of relatives coming meant an emergency visit to the market for groceries. My sons had gone somewhere with their dad, and Lisa and I were accompanied by my then five year old daughter Janel. Janel was not at the age of spelling yet, therefore Lisa and I decided that it was safe to have a few private words together, careful to spell the "secret" words. The conversation started innocently enough with Lisa spelling out the question, then in classic Lisa form, the questions became more ridiculous, purely for the sake of continuing this style of conversation. We had gone way past the point of a secretive conversation and started having a conversation that would have been safe for Janel to hear. We must have kept this silliness up for an hour or more. We laughed so hard over this stupidity that we were almost drunk with laughter. My poor little girl spent the entire shopping experience totally confused by the childlike behavior she was witnessing between her mom and aunt.

Lisa and I spent the majority of our time together during her visit. We did a lot of exciting things while our family was in town. My cousin and her fiancé had never been to the beach before, so we ended up going two days in a row. The children had a beautiful time and so did we, but by far one of our favorite memories of that visit was the silly spelled out exchange between the two of us.

Each of us knows at least one person in our life that we can let our guard completely down with and just give in to the silliness of the moment. If we are fortunate we have more than one. I am fortunate because in my own home I have a group of people always willing to be silly at a moment's notice.

I love the look on my children's face when I wake up on a Saturday morning and decide I want to dance in a chorus line while loudly playing the soundtrack from a Broadway hit; and make them join in. The silliness only gets progressively worse from that point on until I tire our completely and the three of them have to lift me off the floor.

The ability to laugh at ourselves is an important aspect of this journey toward peace. We have many responsibilities that require a more serious side of us. On a daily basis we concern ourselves with the health of our children, job security, making monthly house payments, the responsibilities of intimate relationships and everything in between. Taking a break to be silly just for the heck of it keeps us grounded and brings an element of peace to our lives that we can only get from excessive laughter. Laughter is not only good for the soul, as the popular saying goes; it is also a cheap form of therapy. We should never get so caught up in the everyday problematic situations we encounter, that we lose our ability to do something silly and laugh at ourselves because of it.

If you are going through a state of sadness or extended anxiety, think about the last time you laughed. It is difficult to be sad after a good laugh.

Take Action...

Today, make a date for tea or coffee with your closest friend or relative. Let your guard down and have a ridiculously silly time with them. (This advice works even better if the date you make is with one of your children.) Borrow from Lisa and me and have an entire conversation spelled out. This will not only make you feel better, but the people that are within hearing distance of you will get a good laugh from it as well.

Journey 16

Decide to Be the Bright Spot in Someone Else's Day and You Will Be Blessed For it...

I have a dear friend who has encountered many detours on her journey towards peace. I like to send her text messages in the morning while she is on her way to work and they usually say things like, "Have a beautiful work day", "Be blessed today" and similar messages. I send her these little brighteners with the hope that one will sink in and she will indeed have beautiful days. My friend has a tendency to have bad days and she can never figure out why. It is not unusual for me to ask how her day went and she responds negatively. I love her deeply, but the truth is she expects to have bad days and so she has them. One Monday evening I asked how her day went and she responded that it went well but she expected the work week to go downhill by Friday. Of course by Friday it had gone downhill just as she predicted, or should I say, just as she spoke it into existence. Her negative way of looking at things does not keep me from trying to brighten her day. I realized one day that I get blessed by sending her these constant reminders, so I decided to send her the message, "Decide to be the bright spot in someone else's day and you will be blessed for it."

There are times when we try to find peace and happiness in selfish ways, when really the peace and happiness we are looking for comes from us being the bright spot in someone else's day. I know that we are not responsible for the happiness of others, but being nice to someone when no one else is offering them kindness can do wonders for both people involved.

I am very fortunate to have an unlimited amount of love coming my way every day, but the reality is that I spend the entire day (before my kids come home from school) without having been hugged or kissed and smothered in affection. Unfortunately, many people have no one in their lives that they can count on for daily expressions of love and affection. Believe it or not, the smile you offer to stranger while standing in line at the market maybe the first smile they received all day.

I love the commercial where someone does something nice to help a stranger and then the person who was helped, helps another stranger and it goes on and on. Although that is a commercial to promote a particular product, the sentiment should not be lost on us. When we extend kindness to others it makes them kinder. We may not be the beneficiaries of that kindness but that should not matter. We receive our blessings by being a blessing to others. I strongly believe that the journey towards peace will be a lonely journey unless we decide to bring others along for the ride.

Take Action...

Today and every day, decide to be the bright spot in someone else's day. You will indeed be blessed for it.

Journey 17

Practice Peace through Controlling Your Tongue...

Everything we have ever mastered in life, we mastered because we practiced it over and over again. While on this journey it is important to know that if we are ever to master the art of peace, we need to practice peace. I have a beautiful friend that decided to take this journey with me. I asked her the question one day, "Are you willing to practice peace?" I explained to her that every day I make a conscious decision to be at peace that day. Then after I make the decision to be at peace that day, I do what is necessary to facilitate that peace. There are moments when I fail to achieve peace, but I take the next opportunity to breathe and start again. I am always aware that I am on this journey therefore I am always seeking the opportunity to make different choices than the ones I made prior to my journey.

One of the ways that we can practice peace is to use positive words when speaking to others or when referring to other people. For example, whenever I encounter others whether it is a friendly acquaintance or a stranger, I say words like sweetie or honey or other similar loving words. When I go to a restaurant or other places where people are there to accommodate you, I speak kindly to the staff. I have heard horror stories of famous people going to hotels and restaurants and being cruel to the staff. I work in a field where I encounter people that I have to accommodate and I understand how it feels when someone speaks to you in a manner that could be demeaning. I make sure to use kind words when encountering people in service oriented fields because I know how quickly someone can come along and complain in such a way that it could ruin that persons entire day.

The Bible tells us in the third chapter of James that we need to control our tongue. It goes on to tell us that although the tongue is very small it has the potential to set fires in your life and in the lives of others. Controlling the tongue in a manner that instead of spitting out curses, it praises others takes practice. When our mouths are controlled by evil; jealousy, disorder and selfishness come out. When our mouths are controlled by God and His goodness; mercy, sincerity and consideration of others come out. This takes practice.

I have had days when someone has said something unkind to me and it has affected my entire day. No matter what I did throughout the day I could not shake the words that were spoken to me. Perhaps the reason that I have a hard time shaking this is I am too sensitive, but the truth is that most people are sensitive about things that are said or done to them. Whoever coined the phrase, "sticks and stones may break my bones but words can never hurt me", must have been in a lot of pain and repeated that mantra to them over and over again to get past the hurt. The reality is that words do hurt, but words can heal also. Words can heal nations and closer to home, words can heal our most intimate relationships. We need to be careful how we use the powerful little instrument inside of our mouths.

Practice using kind words. If you are known for speaking to your children harshly, practice using kind words with them. If you are always using words to put your spouse or partner down, practice using kind words to build their character. I know this is a corny little cliché but practice does make perfect.

Take Action...

Today, make a decision to practice peace by controlling the words that come out of your mouth. Before you open your mouth to speak, take a moment to think about what you are about to say before the words come out. Not starting a fire is a lot easier than putting one out, so choose your words very carefully. Many relationships have ended because of the words used by everyone involved. When someone says something to you that hurts, practice forgiveness, knowing that they may not be on their journey towards peace.

Journey 18

Find Pockets Of Peace Wherever You Can...

A few years ago my sister and I were seeking out a place to go on vacation together. She was paying for the trip but told me to pick the place I wanted to go. The very first thing I suggested was a Dude Ranch, but Lisa did not have think that a place without television or wireless Internet was a great idea for a vacation. At the same time my dad was surprising my mom with a cruise to Alaska. Lisa called me up and suggested that we take the cruise with them. Brilliant idea!

I discovered a form of peace on that trip that I had never encountered before. It was during this trip that I discovered the beauty of God's creation. I would love to travel to Alaska whenever I need to be reminded of that sense of peace I felt, but that of course is unrealistic. I have discovered what I call little pockets of peace and it is economical and practical. Whenever I long for Alaska and I need to escape there, I get on the Internet and go to the sites for some of the local papers of the places I visited. Reading the local paper for Sitka or Juneau Alaska makes me feel refreshed. This little pocket sized vacation is the next best thing to being there.

Another example of these little pockets of peace is taking a trip to the local bookstore. The travel section of the bookstore is the best place to visit when the real thing is hard to get to. I have yet to visit a few places that are on my "To Do" list, but I am already in love with these places based on my little pocket of peace vacations. One of the places I virtually visited (prior to actually going) thousands of times is Vermont. I have looked at numerous pictures of trees in Vermont adorned in their finest fall colors. I have taken virtual hikes in the mountains and have walked along a trail around Lake Champlain all while sitting in the aisle at my favorite bookstore. I have walked around Mackinac Island in Michigan and experienced the annual Lilac Festival. I have gone horseback riding in this Equestrian friendly environment and gone on nature walks.

Another way to experience pockets of peace (this will offend a few of you) is to turn your cell phone off. Do not schedule this during the times when your children are at school because in case of emergency your cell phone is essential for contacting you. However any other time you schedule this pocket of peace should suffice. If you are trying to encourage others to take this journey with you, leave a different recording for callers to hear when they try to reach you. Perhaps your message can say something like; "Hello, you have successfully reached me, but you have called at a time when I have turned off my phone and scheduled some peace time for me. Leave a message and after I have returned from this little vacation I will give you a call." This message will let people know that you are valuable enough to yourself that you have scheduled some time for your own well being and it may encourage them to do something similar. This could also open up some much-needed dialog between you and a friend about your journey towards peace.

Take Action...

Today, schedule a pocket of peace. Visit your local bookstore and visit a faraway place. Go on the Internet and read the local paper in a town much different than the one you live in. And for God sake, turn off your cell phone.

Journey 19

Appreciate Yourself...

Appreciate yourself. It seems like such a basic statement, but the truth is that when we speak of all the things in our lives we appreciate, seldom do we say ourselves. It's not that we do not appreciate ourselves, we just tend to think of other things first. We do the same thing when it comes time to being considerate. We tend to consider others first. We have been taught that we should consider others, anything short of that is looked upon as selfish behavior.

We take days off work to tend to sick children, help a friend move and go to scheduled doctor appointments. When was the last time you took a day off to get a massage or a facial? When was the last time you took time off to go to the beach, or hiking or walking on a trail? Schedule some "Me Time" and keep that appointment.

When we appreciate ourselves we are saying that we have value. As we take the journey toward peace, we need to understand how important 'we' are to the journey.

When we do not take time to appreciate our value in relationships, we tend to lose ourselves in that relationship. We need to place our value above the value of everyone we love, by doing this; we have more to offer him or her. If we allow ourselves to place everyone else's needs above our own, when we break down, and we will, they lose also. I love my children so much that I take care of their mom.

There will be days when the needs of others will surpass your own and there will be very little you can do about that. This is the reason why we have to stock up on "me time" so that when we are needed elsewhere, we have a reserve we can borrow from. One weekend in particular, my little ones needed my undivided attention, so I altered my schedule to accommodate them. I had plans that would have kept me away from home, but I altered my plans to make room for John, Travey and Janel. When I left the house, they were with me, and the little work I was able to do, I did between kisses. I kept my bedroom door open, and I was available to kiss various body parts whenever Janel bumped into something (every five minutes). It was a three-day weekend and although I accomplished very little professionally, I gave my children what they needed from their mom. I did not lose any peace over the fact that I got no work done, because I have so much "me time" in reserve that it did not take anything away from me.

Taking time for yourself on a regular basis makes for a better you. When you appreciate yourself, it makes you fully appreciate all the beautiful people you are accountable to as well. Waiting until you are physically and emotionally spent before you take time for yourself is dangerous to your health and happiness as well as a danger to the people around you.

Take Action...

Today, make a decision to schedule some time for yourself. If you are one of those women that live by your appointment book, write your name in your schedule. Take time to be alone and do something that you enjoy. If you are fortunate enough to take this time away from home, take advantage of that. Go to a bookstore and sit in the café enjoying a book that interest you, or take your own book and visit an outdoor café. Whatever you decide to do, make sure it totally benefits you and accommodates your needs. Appreciating yourself may seem selfish, but it is the most loving thing you can do for those you care for.

Journey 20
Make Peace
(Or Live Peacefully)
With Your Quirks...

Quirks a.k.a. odd behaviors, weird habits, insanities.

Quirks... We all have them. Quirks are those little things about us that people find odd or unique. Most of our little quirks can be considered compulsive such as the person who touches food to their chin before placing it in their mouth. Compulsive or not, our little quirks are very much part of who we are and we need to live peacefully with them.

I come from a family of people that are accomplished yet quirky. My beautiful cousin Sabrina is very intelligent. Besides being an educator with a Masters Degree, she single handedly came up with games that are currently being used in several of our state's school districts to help students excel on the statewide exam. Here is the thing, my beautiful, intelligent cousin refuses to learn the words to songs. Every song that comes on the radio is her "favorite" song, yet instead of learning the lyrics, she makes up words that sound similar to the words actually being used. She is extremely content with the artistic ability she has to butcher a perfectly good song. Sabrina is a very good example of one of the quirky people in my family living peacefully with their lunacy.

My sister Lisa is another example of one of the people in my family living peacefully with her quirkiness. Lisa is an accomplished sports director. In addition to making history at a top cable network as their first female sports director, she has also earned five Emmy awards to date. If you were to look at her resume, she would appear to be an intelligent woman. What her resume does not mention is how she spends hours trying to set up the delivery of her favorite salad dressing. HOURS! Lisa has taken a liking to a particular salad dressing that is not available in the state she lives in. She believes that she cannot eat salad without this particular dressing. This salad dressing requires refrigeration so Lisa spent a day coordinating the delivery between the company that makes the product and a widely used delivery service. She had to get the delivery down to a science so that she would be there when it was delivered to her building. Then she spent the next few hours calling everyone she knows to proudly tell them about her perfected delivery setup. A one- time deal like this does not quite classify as a quirk, but she is like this with other snack items as well. She gets extremely excited when Planters comes out with a new flavored almond; she carries an extra suitcase when she visits her friends in Georgia so that she can stock up on flavored water she cannot find in New York. She is fascinated by snack foods so in order to maintain her ideal weight; she spends as much money on gym memberships as she does on her long list of 'favorite' snacks. Lisa lives peacefully with this insanity and makes no excuses for it.

Lisa inherited her quirks from our parents. Our dear, sweet mother; (one of the first to get accepted into the Dental Hygiene school at the local college, after they opened it up to African-Americans), takes pride in being one of those people that knows a lot about so many insignificant things. She is the type of person that you would want to be your lifeline if you ever got accepted to be a participant on one of those game shows. However, this lady still needs map quest to find places in our city, although she has lived here her entire life.

My father may be the worst of all. A respected Building Contractor, first African-American to receive his state contractor's license through examination, yet he will spend an entire work day trying to figure out what color to paint the silly signage that he will place in his vegetable garden. He believes himself to be a great poet/philosopher who goes by the name 'Smythe', and he recently had the great idea to paint a toilet bright red, fill it with soil and plants, and place it in the living room.

These people, whom I happen to be related to, have no problem with who they are. Not only do they find joy in these insanities, they have found a level of peace with their quirks.

Embracing your insanity (quirks) is an important part of your journey. People spend thousands of dollars and countless hours trying to get a Psychiatrist to 'fix' them, rather than come to terms with their beautiful personality flaws.

Some of history's most famous authors, artists and musicians had closets full of odd behaviors and they were able to channel those odd behaviors to form some of their best works.

Take Action...

Embrace the fact that you are a beautiful, intelligent and quirky woman. Instead of spending hundreds of dollars per hour on a Psychiatrist, take half of that money and buy cute shoes, then take the other half and put it in a high interest yielding savings account. The money you save will come in handy when your quirks completely take over and you require full time psychiatric care.

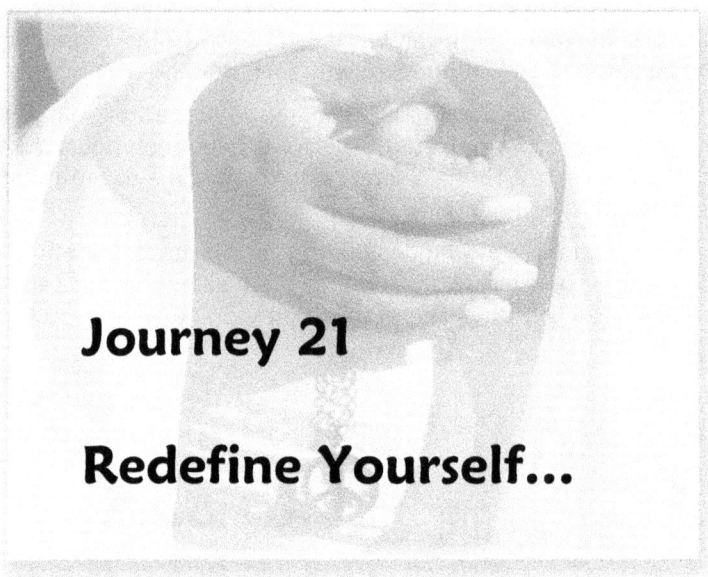

Journey 21

Redefine Yourself...

I love to hear syndicated television psychologist Dr. Phil ask the person he is talking to, how a certain action or behavior is working for them. We get so use to doing things a certain way and even when it's clear that our way of doing things isn't working we continue doing it that way anyway.

I have fallen in to this category of people so many times that it is embarrassing. I am one of those people that tend to hang in there even when it's clear that it is a lost cause. There are many times when I have known to do better and still made the wrong decisions because it was what I was use to doing. There does come a point in our lives that in order to have better results, we will have to act differently. The change needs to come from inside of us and because we are creatures of habit, it may be time to redefine ourselves.

Redefining yourself is a simple concept but difficult in theory. Difficult does not mean impossible though. Imagine that you were looking your name up in a dictionary. What would the current definition say? Are you happy with the definition? If there is something about the current definition that is difficult to read, use your creative powers and ingenuity to rewrite the definition, thereby redefining you. This may sound ridiculous to you, especially if you have never experienced this before, but simply write out who you desire to be and live that way.

I believe there are certain things we are destined to do and we can do very little to change that because that is strictly a God thing; but we can make changes to our character by deciding to do things differently. For example, I know a woman who wanted to make some changes to the policies in her neighborhood. She had no political aspirations whatsoever, but when she found out that a seat was becoming available on her local city commission, she went door to door campaigning for that seat and was elected. She only aspired to stay one term, which was long enough to affect some change, and when her time was up she did not seek re-election.

There are times when redefining ourselves gives us a new appreciation for who we are. When I was born, my mother decided that she wanted a good life for me. She had been working as a Dental Assistant. Shortly after I was born, the Dental Hygiene school at the local college opened up to African-American's and my mother was in the initial class. She made the decision to change her career to provide a better life for me than the one she had growing up. My father had just started his career, and even though it was evident he would be successful at it, my mother felt it was important to make changes in her career for her benefit as well as mine. She was told by several people not to put her new baby in daycare and go to school, but she knew that by doing so, she would provide better for me in the long run.

When I got a little older, my mother decided she wanted to redefine herself all over again. She was offered a position teaching at the very college she had attended. She was so good at what she did that she was asked to teach others who were looking to enter her field. I remember being a little girl and sitting in as my mother taught her students. My mother fascinated me. She captured the attention of her students, held on to their attention throughout class, and when class was over they wanted more of her time. My mother portrayed the type of confidence in front of her class that you can only have when you are at peace with what you are doing.

After three years of teaching, my mother realized that the very trade she had once grown tired of she was missing. She gave up her chalk and textbook manuals, and resumed her career as a Dental Hygienist. Redefining herself made her realize how much she really did enjoy a more hands on approach to her chosen field.

Redefining yourself gives you an opportunity to experience yourself from a different perspective. It also gives you an opportunity to determine what works for you and what does not. As we take this very important journey towards peace, it is important that we gain perspective of what does and does not work in our lives. Perhaps you could use my mom as an example. She did not make a drastic change in her career path; she simply chose to experience it from a different perspective. In doing so, she gained a whole new perspective on her career choice.

As women, we are experts as redefining ourselves. When we make the decision to give up single life and get married; or give up the sports car for the minivan with the infant seat in the back, we are redefining ourselves. When we decide at 36 years old to go back to college, we are redefining ourselves.

In order to be at peace with yourself, you have to be at peace with the choices you make. If the path you continually choose has lead to self-destruction, heartache and suffering, choose a different path. I love the saying; insanity is when we do the same thing over and over again and expect to get a different result each time. Perhaps the change that is needed in your life classifies as huge, but there are usually minor changes that can be made that will redefine you as well. For example, when I grew weary of teaching in the public school system, I accepted a teaching position for the same grade level at a private school. It was a Christian-Military school, which allowed me to be more creative in my teaching style, and I was able to talk to my students about God as well as have morning devotion with them. This minor change in my career (going from public to private school) redefined who I was as a teacher.

Take Action...

Today, write the definition for how you see yourself right now. No one else will ever see this definition because you will destroy it almost immediately after writing it. Read and re-read this definition. How does it make you feel? If you feel great about this honest definition, then your task is simple - keep up the good work. If you do not like the definition you wrote, redefine yourself. Take out another sheet of paper (one that you will keep) and write the definition of who you desire to be. Keep this new definition posted where you can read it every day. It does not matter if it's posted in a place where everyone can see it. After writing this new definition, make the necessary changes to accommodate this new woman you will become.

Let's Pray:

Lord, I come before You today realizing that I have made choices in my life based on who I believed myself to be at the time. This has led to confusion and self - destruction on numerous occasions. But Lord I come to You today asking that You assist me in making an honest evaluation of who I am right now. After that evaluation is written and destroyed, guide me as I make the decisions on whom You need me to be. Direct me as only You can and lead me down a better path, the path that leads to peace.

I thank You right now, in Jesus' name I submit this prayer.

Amen

The Journey to Peace ❧ 91

Journey 22

Peace Interrupted...

While on this journey you will surely find that there will be days when peace, no matter what, will seem to elude you. There will be those days that despite your best effort, everything you think you know about finding peace will escape you. These days are essential toward your journey. Days like this serve as reminders of how important peace is.

Then there are days where your peace will be interrupted because of things that happen naturally like earthquakes, hurricanes, death and other disasters. On days like this it serves our journey better if we embrace the fact that we are truly having a bad day rather than insisting that we have arrived at a point where we can endure anything because of our peaceful state of mind. I encountered days like this on my journey but one particular day stands out among them.

While on my journey I encountered a terrible loss. My beautiful Goddaughter passed away. She was extremely young at the time of her passing, and she passed away painfully. The only bright spot to her painful death was the fact that it ended what was also a very painful life. She was born with a blood disease, Sickle Cell Anemia. She suffered her entire life with this illness and her body gave up after fighting for nineteen years. She was beautiful, intelligent, and kind-hearted and she had a smile that could light up a dark area. I received the call of her death early in the morning. It was devastating. I spent the day pretending to be at peace with everything, feeling this need to be an example of peace for those looking at me. As it turned out, my pretending to be at peace and my sincere struggle to really be at peace with her death made my day anything but peaceful. As it got close to evening I heard this little voice inside of me giving me permission to not be at peace with what happened. No matter where we are on our journey, events such as the loss of someone we love is a great equalizer. It occurred to me that of course it was okay for me to not be okay.

Some of us have made the choice to live inside this little bubble we call inner peace. Truly we do avoid some of the pitfalls others encounter because of the path we chose, but every now and then that little bubble gets penetrated by events that are devastating to us. Our level of peace gets interrupted and we have to be strong enough to accept that we do not always have to be strong. I was looking to be at peace at a time when it was okay for me not to be.

I learned something very important from that experience. We have to have a level of peace that prevents us from a relapse even when we experience a devastating loss. The journey towards peace is a journey that we take step by step every day. We will arrive at what we think is the end of our journey only to find that we are not even halfway there. We do however, need to maintain a level of peace that will help us to deal effectively with those days when peace eludes us or our peace gets interrupted.

Take Action...

Today, embrace the fact that there are days when our peace will be interrupted. If our peace is interrupted because of loss, we should understand that it is okay for us to not handle things so well. Mourning our loss is an appropriate response, resisting the need to mourn is a waste of energy and we are simply delaying the inevitable.

Journey 23
Peace Under Fire
(Maintaining Your Grace)...

The world as we know it, tends to change without our permission. Behaving gracefully under the harshest of circumstances is difficult and can be a true test of our faith.

I met a man that I befriended at the lowest point in his life. Raul started his day just like any other day; busy. This is a man who wakes up running and it takes a lot to slow him down. At the point in the day when he should have been preparing himself to rest, he got a phone call that shook his world and tested his faith. His sister-in-law Donna had to place the call to him letting him know that his daughter Giselle and her mother Michele were brutally killed in their home by a cowardly monster (who I will refer to as satan in this chapter).

Donna, (who is Michele's sister and Giselle's aunt), was left with the difficult task of notifying her mom Nancy and her other sister Janice. This was the most horrific thing this family had ever endured. As expected there was always an underlying anger that they all shared toward satan. Of course there was a strong sadness; one would expect that. What caught me by surprise were the other things I noticed about them.

Raul, at the lowest point in his life, was loving, generous and patient. Donna maintained a strength and balance that was admirable, and Nancy and Janice were graceful and kind. This family had every reason and every excuse to behave bitterly but at the lowest point in their lives they maintained peace and grace.

Not too long after the world changed for the Vinas and Wallace family, the world changed again. This time it was a little closer to home.

My God-brother Jay, was a Security Officer for the United Nations. He lost his life to a terror attack in Afghanistan. He died a hero. Jay had many opportunities to get away with his own life but he died saving the lives of over 20 other people. He died as he attempted to go back to save one more. Jay was only 27 years old.

Words cannot describe the level of faith and peace that his mother Sandra had during the most difficult time of her life. Sandra has always been a woman of grace and her faith in God is unquestionable. Even at a time when she had to remind herself to breathe, she never had to remind herself to believe. My own mother and father, who loved Jay as a son, leaned on God and leaned on the strength of character that Jay showed even in his last moments.

The one thing that I know for sure that the Maxwell, Wallace and Vinas families share is a strong faith in God. I strongly believe that what enables us to maintain peace under fire is a strong faith. The love, generosity and grace that these families showed can only come from the peace of God that surpasses all of our understanding.

96 ~ Carol Watson

Take Action...

Today, hug the people you love and tell them just how much you love them.

Journey 24

Enjoy The View...

Sometime ago I made a last minute decision to take a 26-hour road trip with two of my friends, Keia and Jenny, from Miami, Florida to St. Catherine's Ontario, Canada. My two friends were going to Canada for an American Thanksgiving and I was invited to go along. Jenny is from St. Catherine's and we were staying with her family. She had taken this road trip before but neither I nor Keia had ever done anything like this. We all taught at the same school and worked a full day before getting in the car and taking the trip. I was exhausted even before we got out of Florida, and we still had about 20 hours to go. It was gonna be a long ride.

The road trip took us into states I had never visited before. It was November, the day before Thanksgiving and the further north we drove, the colder it became. I have always enjoyed cold weather more than anything else and this trip was no different. We were all bundled up in the car and enjoying every moment of it. We got into West Virginia as the sun was coming up and the sunlight allowed us to enjoy the beautiful view. I was taking in the beauty of the mountains and I was fascinated with driving through the tunnels. Just when I thought West Virginia could not get more beautiful, we ran into snow- covered grounds. We were following a carefully mapped out route, which led us down some back roads, which would lead us to the perfect highway, to keep us going in the right direction. On one of those back roads we came across snow. It had not snowed very heavy, but it was enough snow to cover the grounds, and for a couple of girls from Miami it was very exciting. We came across a ranch with beautiful horses in the front yard. I love snow and I love horses, so we pulled over for a photo opportunity. I took pictures in front of the house with the horses standing in the snow as my background. We spent the rest of our journey less concerned about the long ride ahead, and more fascinated by the view. The further we drove, the more beautiful it became and the closer we were to our destination. I spoke to my dad he cautioned me to drive carefully through the snow. When traveling in conditions unfamiliar to you it is great advice to be cautious, but we were driving both slow enough to enjoy the view, and fast enough to get across the Canadian border in time to get a good night sleep.

With every journey, regardless of the destination it is good advice to travel carefully, being careful to not fall into traps unfamiliar to you, but as you do so, it would benefit you greatly to enjoy the view along the way. The things we see as we travel are part of the trip. I have taken many road trips through Florida and each time I am still fascinated by the beauty of our great state. The orange groves, the little hidden rivers I see as I drive along the interstate between Miami and Daytona Beach. I am always happy to get where I am going, but I always enjoy the view along the way.

E. Claudette Freeman gave me some great advice at the start of writing this book. She told me to be careful to notice all the things around me. She was telling me to begin to notice all the beauty that I am surrounded with on a regular basis. I began to notice things on my usual routes that I had never seen before. I like going to the beach on a regular basis, usually early in the morning or late in the evening. My route to the beach takes me through my favorite part of town, downtown Hollywood, Florida. There is a very popular park in downtown where the city puts on a lot of free concerts and events. On my way home from the beach one morning I noticed a very large and colorful butterfly sculpture had found its home in the park. It may have been there for months, but I had never noticed it before. I immediately called Claudette and thanked her for the advice she had given the day before. It was because of my conscious effort to notice my surroundings had I noticed this beautiful piece of art.

As we journey towards peace, it is important that we enjoy the view along the way. What we encounter along the way is an essential part of the journey. The very last line in the piece I wrote about Peace says; "I am on my journey to find her and I find her at every turn along the way." That line best describes the benefits of enjoying the view. There are little pockets of peace that we encounter everyday of our lives but we have to be aware of their existence. We need to take notice of the things we come across everyday because surely throughout the routine of the day we have missed something very essential to our journey.

Take Action...

Today, utilize the advice that was given to me. As you travel your usual routes and live your lives day to day, take notice of the things that have been there the whole time. We are surrounded by things that will bring us contentment, happiness and peace, if only we take notice of them. Today as you travel your usual routes and do your routine things, take notice. It is amazing what you will find along the way. As you take this journey towards peace, enjoy the view.

Journey 25

Make Peace With The Knowledge That You May Have To Take Your Journey Alone...

When I started my journey I was certain that the people closest to me would embrace the concept of living peacefully. I believed that once they embraced the idea of living a life of peace, they too would take this journey with me. I was relieved to come across so many women ready to take the journey, but I was very disappointed to find that some were not as fascinated with living peacefully. Once you begin your journey, you become conscious of two sets of people; the ones who are ready and the ones who refuse. If you are fortunate enough you will find yourself surrounded by people that want to take the journey with you, but be ready to take the journey alone if need be. The journey towards peace is easier when you have companions to accompany you, however it is not impossible to take the journey alone.

I met a woman who lives in a desperately depressing situation. She is married to a man who is verbally abusive at his best. In addition to the verbal abuse, he does not work and she finds herself working very hard to maintain their family financially. Even in the midst of her situation, she is determined to take this journey. Every day is a struggle but she is dedicated to living peacefully.

It is very difficult to make a lifestyle change when the challenge is as close to home as your own spouse. Many women have similar experiences spiritually, when they make a decision to join a church or become more active at church. If their husbands are not churchgoers it is likely that the wives will receive ridicule at home. It is not uncommon to hear women talk about the negativity they received at home when they made efforts to improve their lifestyles, whether it is a better job, continuing education, weight loss, or gain, or other changes for the better. There are men who become insecure with the thought that if you make improvements in your life, you may decide you are too good for them. Because these changes are for your own good, you must be determined to move in the right direction regardless of the resistance you receive at home.

I do not make light of this at all, and I fully understand the difficulty and disappointment involved in living in a situation like this. I will however say this, it is not impossible and the resistance you receive while on this journey will make the reward even sweeter. Find peace in this; when taking the journey with someone else, they may begin to feel that whatever gain you make is because you have them with you, but when you journey alone, the honor belongs only to you and God.

You may find yourself in a situation such as described above or like me you may find that on some days you have company on your journey and on some days you have none at all. The days when I have company on my journey I find that it is easier and of course the other days are more difficult. Difficult does not mean impossible. On those days, I dig in my heels and I resume my journey.

Take Action...

Today, determine to take your journey regardless of who takes it with you. I admit that it is difficult, but like I stated before, difficult does not mean impossible. If you are going to gain ground on this journey, you will have to find peace with the fact that you may have to take the journey alone.

Journey 26

Determine Your Destination...

For as long as I can remember, I had a desire to visit the great state of Vermont. I am not sure when I decided that I just had to visit there, but my decision was made and I was determined to go. I would often mention to people that I planned on visiting there one day but no one expressed interest in going along. Finally, I met a beautiful adventurous person (Michelle) who never had plans on visiting Vermont, but figured it was worth a try. We scheduled our visit for November, and decided to arrive in Vermont on Thanksgiving Day.

In the months leading up to our visit, I virtually visited Vermont on the Internet and at the bookstore. I looked at maps of Vermont and I looked at maps of Burlington, the city we were visiting. I learned everything I needed to know about Burlington. I learned where the best hotel was located to accommodate my desire to be near Lake Champlain. I learned where the closest Starbucks and bookstore were located. I knew exactly where the best shopping was and the bicycle shop to rent bikes to ride the trail around the lake. I called the local visitors bureau to get tidbits of info and because we were coming in on Thanksgiving Day, I called around to see which restaurants would be open and serving Thanksgiving Dinner. I did everything a person does while they anxiously await the trip they have always dreamed of taking.

I did everything short of making an itinerary, because in my experience the best made plans usually go array. I did however have enough information to know what was available to do when I was not shivering cold, eating, relaxing or hiking. I had determined my destination and made my game plan. I was ready to visit the great state of Vermont.

Whenever you visit a new place, face a new challenge, or venture into unknown territory, it is best to determine your destination. When facing a new challenge, even when it is not planned or desired, it is smart to determine what you wish to gain from the experience. Even when facing difficulties, it is best to make a game plan and pay attention to the lessons you are learning along the way. Determining your destination could mean that you will not be powerless in determining the outcome of the situation.

When making my plans to go to Vermont it was important that I did my research. Had I not done my research I would have arrived in Burlington and spent hours trying to find a restaurant that would be open on Thanksgiving; only to later find that the only open restaurant was the one in the hotel.

As much as I looked forward to biking around the lake, I would have been disappointed to discover that the bike shop needed a two day notice to get the bikes out of storage and ready for the rental, due to the fact that not many bikes get rented in the winter and they were stored away for the season. Making plans, even if they have to be altered later, make for a better outcome.

Determining your destination can determine your outcome. Years ago when the Clintons left the White House and made their home in New York, it was widely known that it was for political reasons. Everyone from the media to average people like me knew that Bill and Hillary were making arrangements to be in the best place to advance Hillary's political career. It came as little surprise when she sought the Senate seat for New York and later she declared her run for the top office in the United States. Long before the Clinton's left the White House, it could be said that Hillary was determining her destination.

When I began my journey towards peace, it did not come without obstacles. In my experience, (and I am sure you can relate) whenever I decide to do the right thing, I am tempted with wrong. We have probably all heard the sayings: whenever I desire to do good, evil is always present or whatever can go wrong will... In other words, if you have decided to take this journey, you must know that it will not come without challenges. By determining where you desire to be, you have a greater chance of reaching your destination. I am always aware that I am on this journey. Even on those days when I lose focus of where I am, I am always aware of where I am going. The knowledge of my destination keeps me focused and it gets me back on track when I have fallen down or taken a detour.

My personal goal as I journey towards inner peace is to be a better person, a better mom and a better companion. I want my sister Lisa to have as good of a sister as I have, I want my children to know that adopting them was one of the smartest decisions I ever made. Inner peace is simply a means to an end. The destination is becoming a better citizen of this great place we live in.

Take Action...

Today, if you have not already done so, determine your personal destination. What is it that you hope to gain from this journey? The obvious answer of course is inner peace, but there should be more you seek to find along the way. Perhaps like me, you desire to be a better person or a better mom. Maybe you desire to be a better employee or a better boss. Whatever it is, once you determine your destination, you are also determining your outcome.

Journey 27

Practice Peace by Showing Compassion...

In relationships I have found it most difficult to deal with someone who lacks sympathy, empathy and compassion. I can recall thinking how different things would be between whomever, and me if only they could understand how I feel, or vice versa.

I met someone who I became very close to. When we met she told me stories about an old friend that had really hurt her in the past. Our friendship was rocky at best and after a while she did the same things to me that had been done to her. I told her that she was treating me in the same manner that she had been treated previously, but because it had been some years since her experience, she had forgotten what it felt like to be hurt. I asked her over and over to reconsider her actions, but she was very cold and unconcerned. She lacked the compassion that one human being should have for another. To make matters worse, at the same time she was showing me this side of her, she was seeking a position that would require her to relate to others and show compassion for other people's needs. I questioned her sincerity for the position, because in my experience she lacked what was necessary to be successful in that role.

Compassion is unselfish. It is relating to another on the level where they are, not on the level you want them to be. The search for peace should not be for selfish reasons. As you grow gracefully, it should be for the benefit of others as well. No one is going to care about your journey towards peace if every time you open your mouth your words are cold and calculating. With your growth, a change for the better should occur as well.

For example, if you are tither at church and you have a job that pays $1,000.00 per week, $100.00 is going to your church every week for tithes. The day you get a promotion and an increase in pay, you stand before the church and talk about how good God is and how He elevated you in your career. Now instead of $1,000.00 per week, you are earning $2,000.00. When you pay your tithes however, you are still giving $100.00 instead of $200.00. What is the benefit to the church if you get an increase but it does not trickle down to the church?

As we journey toward peace, we should do so with the mindset that as we grow, we need to be a blessing to others as well. The knowledge we gain on the way, we should use to elevate others who are going through tough times. We were not always where we are today and for all we know there could be a pit waiting for us to fall into tomorrow. The compassion we show to others when they need it will be available to us when we need it. Compassion is reciprocal.

I strongly believe that there is a direct connection between inner peace and global peace. I live with the impression that people who live peacefully do not promote war. When we are compassionate we promote change. I live in the United States, a country that has not experienced war on our own soil in my lifetime. When I send my children to school I do not live in fear of suicide bombers walking into their school and ending their lives. My little ones are not exposed to American soldiers walking up and down the street with assault weapons ready for battle. I feel strong emotions for mothers in war torn countries that send their children to a market and worry if they will ever see them again.

When we embrace peace, that peace should spread to others. We will show compassion for the people around us that are struggling with issues that are important to them. We have a bad habit of only feeling emotion when the very thing we have ignored in someone else's life comes knocking our door down. I feel as though if we show compassion towards others when they are struggling with an issue, we are less likely to experience that same issue. We do not want God to start placing us in a position where we learn firsthand how others are feeling.

Our ability to show compassion is one of the things that separate us from sociopaths.

Take Action...

Today and everyday take notice to what the people around you are going through. When someone we care about exposes their suffering to us, the most loving thing we can do for them is offer them a compassionate ear and compassionate words. Imagine what you would need to hear if you were in the same or similar situation and then do that. Placing yourself in another person's shoes and then treating them accordingly is the essence of compassion.

Journey 28

Maintain Your Spiritual Health, It Is Essential To Your Journey...

"Peace is a necessary condition of spirituality, no less than an inevitable result of it."
— Aldous Huxley

There have been days when I feel as though I cannot find my equilibrium. I spend the morning off balance, off target and totally unorganized. I would often think that my lack of balance had everything to do with missing out on my morning shot of caffeine. When I finally roll into Starbucks and grab a cup of coffee, it does very little to alter my state of being. I am usually well into the evening before I realize that I woke up in such a hurry that I neglected to pray or read my bible. I end up losing an entire day because I neglected to feed my spirit.

Maintaining spiritual health is essential to this journey. Regardless of your religious beliefs, it is important to maintain them. When we neglect to eat nutritious foods, our physical body becomes weak. The same concept applies to our spiritual body. What we do not feed we destroy.

Prior to my very serious walk with God, I was the type of Christian that would pick up my bible only on my way to church. When I got back home, I would put my bible back in its place and that's where it would stay until the next Sunday. I had a habit of only praying to God when the Pastor would lead us in a uniformed prayer or when I was under a great amount of stress. During this time I never noticed any spiritual imbalance or consequences to not acknowledging God. However once my walk became closer to Him, my responsibility to Him became greater. Now when I do not take the time to acknowledge God through study or prayer, He tends to make my day uneasy. It's not a curse that He places on my life to make my day go not so great, it's just a gentle reminder that I need Him to make my way easier.

Like most women who have decided to take the journey to peace, a life filled with despair and disappointment is what led me to seek inner peace. Seeking God is essential to turning things around in our lives so that we either will not have to face the same challenges we did in the past, or not have to face them alone. There are so many things I deal with on a regular basis that can take away from my level of peace. Maintaining my inner peace during those times totally depends on whether or not I have sought after God on that day. I do not always handle things the way I am suppose to spiritually, so I am thankful for the reminders I get to pursue God.

Every woman on this journey will find her own way to maintain balance, but as for me I find that there is very little peace without God.

Take Action...

Today, write down all the ways you acknowledge God. If your page is empty, you may have just uncovered what hinders your peace.

Let's Pray:

God, today I come before You with the knowledge that I can do very little on this journey without You. I know that You alone are the God of peace and no journey to inner peace could begin or continue without You. I do not always enjoy the reminders you give me to acknowledge You and trust You, but I do appreciate those reminders because they constantly draw me back to You, my one true and only source of peace and strength. Thank you God that You love me enough to want to hear my voice every day.

In Jesus' name I submit this prayer.

Amen.

Journey 29

Embrace Peace...

"Give peace a chance."

John Lennon

Peace is a choice; some choose it, while others do not.

I am certain that all of us know someone who we could describe as confrontational. It seems that no matter what we try when dealing with this person, they will always choose to handle things adversely. I did business with just such a person. I will call this person 'Polly'. No matter what I said to Polly, she would tend to take the opposite stance. I had a theory that she did not have a true stand on anything except the desire for confrontation and debate. I tested my theory. I had previously stated my opinion about something to Polly, and she of course felt the opposite. A few weeks later, I brought up the same scenario, except on that occasion, I took the side she had taken weeks before. True to form she negated me by taking the exact stand I had taken before. I tested my theory a few other times, mostly because I enjoyed it so much and partly to see if she would always react the same way. She proved me right time after time. I realized that she did not stand for anything other than opposition.

In another incident, I unwittingly did something to her that involved a business dealing. It was not intentional and because of the way it occurred, it should have been obvious that it was an accident. I became aware of the problem after business hours during a time when I was unable to rectify it. I did however take care of the matter within the first hour of business the next day. I apologized to her for my error, but she refused the apology. I was left with the impression that she would rather I did not resolve the issue so that she would have had a valid reason to behave in a manner that was comfortable to her. By resolving the issue and apologizing for my error, I took away her ammunition and I truly believe that annoyed her. She called again about a week later for the sake of business, but never made mention of the ugly things she said or her refusal to accept my apology.

With peace we have two options. We can either promote it or reject it. What we receive in life in way of blessings depends on which stance we take. To live a life that pleases God, we need to always choose peace. When we truly embrace peace we will be blessed with the very things that come along with it; Happiness, love, serenity, sanity...

Within my family I have been blessed to have women in my family that are role models for embracing peace. One example is my aunt Audrey. My aunt has suffered great loss in the last few years, which culminated with the loss of her oldest daughter Allegra. My cousin Allegra was diagnosed with a very aggressive form of cancer and although she fought it very bravely, God had a different plan. When Allegra passed away, she left behind three very young children and my Aunt Audrey is now being a mother to her grandchildren.

Prior to my Aunt's life going from bad to worse, she had to deal with a very difficult person. Prior to my uncle Freeman meeting Audrey, he had three beautiful children from another woman. These three children along with his other kids are the joy of his life, but their mom battled Audrey with everything she had in her. Audrey never said a word. No matter what she did to Audrey, she held her peace and continued to take care of my uncle Freeman, her kids, his kids and their grand children. Audrey maintained a level of dignity and respect that can only come from inner peace. Audrey would have had every excuse to act ugly, but she never lost her composure. If she had acted out, everyone would have understood, but instead she embraced peace.

There will be times (many times) when we will be confronted with the opportunity to either blow our stack or embrace peace. We will not always make the right choice. Let me rephrase that, "I do not always make the right choice". Whenever we fail to embrace peace we have a responsibility to ourselves and to this journey, to pick ourselves up, dust off our knees and elbows (or chins, if like me you often fall on your face), forgive ourselves and keep moving forward.

The journey we are on is certainly not easy but it is worth it. If you have not already been tested while on this journey, no doubt you will be. Shortly after I consciously started my journey I encountered a financial crisis. I am sure that you know that nothing can interfere with your level of peace more than a health scare or worrying about how you will feed your children. I did not always recognize my crisis as a test of my faith on this journey, but I do know now that a test was all it was. God will always come through on our behalf. The only crisis we cannot recover from is our own death, everything else is temporary.

There were so many days I had to remind myself of my journey. I would post visual reminders everywhere. Everywhere I looked there were reminders of the journey that I am on. I wore a necklace with the peace symbol on it. Every time I would look in the mirror, there was a reminder. My bracelet had a peace symbol; my belt buckle had one as well. I eventually went so far as to have the symbol tattooed on the inside of my wrist.

We must do all we can to embrace peace in our lives. The peace we create on the inside of us is directly connected to the peace we will create around us.

Take Action...

Today, make a decision to embrace peace whenever you are presented with the choice. Without a doubt this is an effort that may take many tries, but keep trying anyway.

Journey 30

Expose Yourself...

Often while I am asleep I hear from God. He tends to use those hours when I am asleep to talk to me. In my opinion He uses that time because it's the only time He is guaranteed to get my undivided attention. Usually He talks to me about me and He is either reprimanding me or giving me wisdom for my journey, but on this particular night He spoke to me about someone else. God decided to speak to me about someone who I can only admire from afar off, Oprah Winfrey.

God spoke to me and He said, "Carol you know what makes Oprah (God just calls her by her first name) admirable? Her ability to be transparent." Talk about an ah-hah moment. I adore Ms. Winfrey, but I do not think I ever thought about her transparency being the reason she is so admired. Although she is a favorite topic of the tabloids, she leaves very little to the imagination. She is as exposed as a fully dressed person can be.

There is something very free about being exposed. People have spent tons of money and energy keeping their secrets hidden only to have them come to the light anyway. As a Christian I believe in God and satan. I was at a conference some years ago. I cannot recall the entire scope of the conference but I recall something significant being said by one of the speakers. What she said has stayed with me ever since. She said something along the lines of this; when satan rears his ugly head and tries to blackmail you with a little secret, don't try to force him back into a closet, expose him. Exposing the very thing that satan is trying to hold over you, frees you from his stronghold. Ah-hah! Before that day I never once thought about that. There is peace involved in living exposed. No one can hold your mistakes over your head because of your fear of being found out. Of course living exposed leaves us vulnerable to ridicule, but we gain more than we lose by living in the light.

I love that point we reach in relationships where we can trust our partner with our most guarded secrets. The capability to open up and expose ourselves to our partner can free us to be who we desire to be.

One day Michelle decided to tell me about her phobia. Prior to this day, I often thought she was nuts. We would go to a restaurant and she would tell me where to sit. I later found out that because of her crazy phobia (I call it a phlobia; I added the 'l' for lunacy), she could only sit in certain spots. She cannot sit next to the wall, or in a booth, or on a chair that has a blemish (I did mention it was a crazy phobia, right?) She had never shared this craziness with anyone else, but once she told me about it, it freed her up. Now whenever we go to a restaurant, we both laugh as she searches for the perfect spot to sit.

On this journey we will find many obstacles. There are so many things that occur that are unavoidable on our part. The best approach to handling these issues is to take better control over the things that are under our control. The more ammunition we take away from satan and his little followers, the more energy we will have to deal with the issues that require our attention. There are many aspects to this journey toward peace. There are many components that need to be in place in order for us to be successful on this journey. Living exposed is as important as any other part of the journey.

Take Action...

Today, take inventory of the areas in your life that are holding you back because of your fear of exposure. Make a decision to live your life exposed. This is very important, but I will pray that you be cautious. There are some secrets that could be dangerous if exposed, so seek counsel before exposing certain things. If you for instance have a secret that if exposed could put you in danger, then no amount of advice from a book should be your final solution. Seek the aid of a spiritual leader about your individual situation. Your first duty should be your safety and the safety of your children. After you have taken every precaution to ensure your safety, by all means... live in the light.

Journey 31

Practice Peace by Showing Love...

Love is stronger than hate. There are those that disagree with me when I say this and I understand why. Hate appears to be stronger because when people hate, they have no difficulty displaying those feelings. When someone hates you, they tell you, and they show you. People hang flags in front of their homes that display hate and they place bumper stickers on the back of their vehicles with hateful words directed towards certain ethnic groups. As a little girl I remember a time I was riding in the car with my mom. We got to a red light and in front of us was a big open bed truck with a confederate flag waving off the back of it. The person had the words, "let the south rise again," painted on the back of the truck. At the time I did not know what the flag represented and I certainly did not know what "let the south rise again" meant, but I remember being bothered by it. That individual and others like him have no problem expressing their hate.

When we are angry with someone we do not hold back our feelings. We use looks that call for the expression, "If looks could kill." We use hateful words, we toss clothes out of windows, slash tires, break windows, knock holes in walls, hang up the phone while the other person is still talking, ignore the person's repeated phone calls, file false police reports of abuse, empty bank accounts, end relationships, file for divorce... The list can go on and on. On the other hand, when we love someone, we say "I love you" and go on about our day. We send flowers on a birthday or Valentine's Day, and we tend to take for granted that this individual just knows how we feel.

It is not difficult to understand why people live with the belief that hate is the stronger emotion. Love is the stronger emotion and when expressed and acted upon the results of that love can be profound.

When I first met my little girl, she was a month old. She was the tiniest little person I had ever seen. A social worker brought her to my home. She had her in a carrier when she handed her over to me and I was afraid to take her out. Janel had this skin that looked like it would tear if I touched her. She was born prematurely and her biological mother used drugs and alcohol while pregnant with her, so the combination of all these factors made her very fragile.

Shortly after Janel came home I took her to the pediatrician. He was the same doctor I took my boys to and I trusted him and his opinion. He discussed with me the difficulties I would have with Janel within the first few months and possibly the first two years. I was facing issues with Janel having difficulties sleeping and the possibility of crib death. Needless to say I had many nights when I did not sleep simply because I kept waking up to check on her breathing. Janel slept, I did not.

About a week after I got my little baby a well intended social worker came to our home to tell me that when Janel was a few months old I could send her to this daycare/intervention center for babies born with drugs and alcohol in their blood. This program was going to be perfect for Janel. Getting into this program would mean that when she was old enough, she would automatically get into the Head Start program, which was a program with a very long waiting list at the time. I really wanted my baby to get into that program. Janel was not going to be eligible for the daycare center until she was about four months old. Instead of sitting around the next few months waiting for daycare, I did what every other mom would do, and then some. I held my baby, read to her, I sang to her, massaged her little bones, and did little exercises with her to loosen up her muscles. I went against the doctor's orders and put cereal in her formula to fatten my little baby up. I slept with her on my chest so that she could feel my heart beat while we were asleep. Janel was being surrounded by love 24 hours a day. Over the next few months she grew into this tough little cookie that was quite different than the little baby they first handed over to me. I took her to the doctor for a checkup and he asked me what happened to the baby he had seen a few months ago. It took some convincing for me to assure him that this was the same little girl he had seen a couple of months before. He was less concerned with the health issues he had previously spoken to me about.

Shortly after the doctors visit, the social worker came back to do the paper work needed to get Janel into the daycare center. After the visit from the social worker, a physical and an occupational therapist, I was informed that Janel no longer qualified for the program. Instead of simply existing, she was thriving. We loved her to health. I wanted my baby in that program because of the long- term benefits involved with her enrollment, but the love we poured on her in those months created a healthy environment for her to grow in. My baby no longer qualified for a program for unhealthy babies.

Love is powerful when acted upon and useless when it sits idle. My son John was two years old when he came to live with me. I was single at the time and I was taking on a very difficult task as a single parent. When John's caseworker first told me about him I wanted to run in the opposite direction. He was currently in a foster home but the foster mother wanted him out. He had only been in the foster care system for a year, but within that time he had been in 16 different foster homes. I love that son of mine, but I must say that when I first met him he had the social skills of someone who had been raised by wolves. He was sweet somewhere underneath it all, but it was hard to look past the outward displays of wild behavior. The caseworker pretty much begged me to not ask them to move him out of my home if I agreed to take him in. They gave me exactly 24 hours to make a decision as to whether or not to take him in. After much prayer I decided to do it. It took me about 48 hours after he moved in to realize that I loved him and after that love was realized it was just a matter of showing him. Prior to knowing I would be getting a child, I had a plane ticket to go see my sister Lisa in Atlanta for a one-week visit. I told the caseworker about it before John moved in and they told me that the week I was gone they would arrange for alternate care for him. After I got John, I was not comfortable with the concept of sending him somewhere else for a week while I vacationed. I made the decision to take him with me. The agency had to give me written consent to take him, but I had to pay the $200.00 plane fare. I took him with me.

He was such a pleasure to travel with that strangers on the plane were asking me what my secret to parenting was. I just smiled because I knew that I had no clue what I was doing. I just loved the heck out of that little boy. John was so well behaved there was no place I would go that I could not take him. He blossomed under my care. I just kept loving him. I told him I loved him, I hugged him, I dealt with him gently at bath time, enduring his screams at the fear of being held underwater (one of the many abuses he had endured in his young life) The more I loved him and protected him from harm, the more he trusted me and he rewarded me by being the best kid I could imagine. My co-workers fought over who would baby-sit John. He was the ideal kid. He went from being shy and withdrawn to being arrogant and self-confident. My mother said to me on many occasions that because of the way I loved John, he went from being a child that no one wanted to a child that everyone wanted. To this day, John still has no problem jumping in my lap for a hug and a kiss and he is the only one of my children to be arrogant enough to just open the bedroom (or bathroom) door and come in without permission or an invitation. He displays love to others in a way that could have only been learned through action not just words.

Actively loving my children has taught me the benefits of what love can do when not just spoken but acted upon. We should never take for granted those that we love. We cannot expect love to thrive if we merely speak it without putting it into action. We practice peace by showing love to others. My children still want to hang out with me after I chastise them because no amount of words I use when I discipline them outweighs the acts of love I display every day. The peace that we encounter at home is largely based on the love we practice in the home. The peace we encounter outside the home will be largely based on the love we display to others around us.

Take Action...

Today, take inventory of your relationships. The people that you are saying I love you to; are you simply saying it, or is the proof in the pudding? If you find after an honest evaluation that you are not displaying love, make a conscious decision to exhibit love. Love is indeed the stronger emotion but we must promote that belief by our actions.

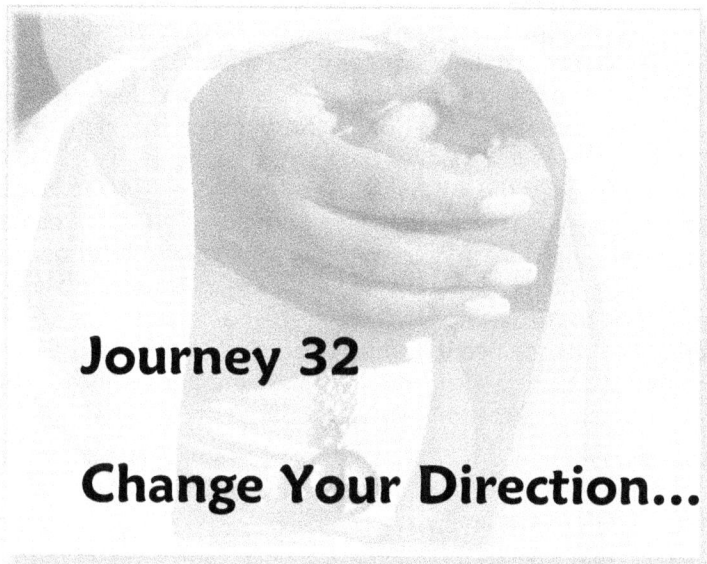

Journey 32

Change Your Direction...

Many times in our lives we see ourselves going in one direction when it is clear we should be going the other way. The Interstate in Miami gets jammed during rush hour. Many times I have gotten on the expressway and right away I realize my mistake. Rather than wait it out, sometimes I get off and take a different route to my destination. There have been times however when regardless of the traffic I stay on the Interstate and ride at a snail's pace. What if the alternate route is even worse than the one I am currently on? Often my reason for staying is I am unfamiliar with the alternative routes.

I sometimes take the same approach with my life. I am aware that the direction I am headed in or the route I am taking is causing my life to move at a snail's pace. I am afraid however to take a chance at an alternative. Many times (too many to mention) I have hindered myself from growth because of fear.

There are many women who live without this fear, but there are many still that do. When we refuse to make changes in our life, we are choosing to become extinct. Changing the course of our life could be the difference between existing and thriving. The days I choose to live and thrive rather than simply try to make it through the day; are the days I find the most peace.

My Aunt Edith fell madly in love in high school with a handsome guy. Not too long after she graduated she married him and had a little girl. Rather than finish college she decided to get a job to support herself and my cousin Sabrina. Over the next few years she had several jobs but none were affording her the lifestyle she wanted for the two of them. After a while Auntie Edith decided to go back to college and finish the degree she had began a few years earlier. After successfully earning her Bachelors degree, she earned her Master's degree as well. She managed to earn both degrees while raising a family and working full time as an Educator. Making the decision to change her direction afforded a better life for herself, Sabrina and her younger daughter Chantal. Making the choice to change her direction also gave her the financial stability to walk away from an unsuccessful marriage.

I have always known my Aunt Edith to be beautiful and confident, but there is a certain amount of confidence that is gained by making a better life for your family.

You may find while on your journey, that you are going in the wrong direction. I have been tested time and time again, and there have been times when I have failed. Instead of following the map or guide, I have strayed off on my own following my emotions. When I have gotten angry, anxious or depressed, these emotions have led me in the opposite direction of where I should be. I recall a time when I lost my direction and got turned around. Rather than journey toward peace my life had taken a 180-degree turn and I ended up heading back where I started. I was having a difficult time finding my way towards peace. Finally I came to realize that somewhere along the way I had lost my direction. I had to change my attitude and refocus my attention back on the positive things that promoted peace in my life. I was going through a difficult time and feeling sorry for myself. Rather than dealing effectively with things I was focusing all my attention on self- pity. I had to change my attitude, change my approach and thereby change my direction.

A change in direction could be as simple as choosing to go to college like my Aunt Edith or changing careers. It could also be a matter of changing the physical state you live in like my sister Lisa. It could mean changing your state of mind.

Changing your direction could mean finding your way out of a traffic jam. It could also mean finding a way out of the jams we get ourselves into. We gain the most from life when we take chances. When things are not being accomplished based on the path you are on, change your path.

Take Action...

Today, rather than wait for another new year to roll around to make resolutions; resolve today to change your direction. You may feel that your life is already headed in the right direction. Great job! However if you are like me and you know you need to make some changes, a change of direction is essential. Make a list of the areas in your life that require a new direction. Put each item on a separate sheet of paper then carefully map out what you need to do to facilitate the changes. The possibilities for change are only limited to your unwillingness to change.

Journey 33

Live Simply...

Life can get complicated. I have heard ministers say; God never said it would be easy, He just promised to be by our side. That news may be comforting to some, and on some days I am myself comforted by that knowledge. However there are days when I need both; an easy day and God by my side. There have been so many times when I have sat around feeling sorry for myself. I have spent time focusing on my problems or whatever I may feel is 'complicating' my life at that moment. When I take the time to think (realistically) about my situation, I often realize that I got myself into it. For the most part, the things that most complicate our lives are based on material possessions. If you were to look at your credit report you would most likely find that your debt is based on your need for material gain. Lines of credit for purchases at department stores, expensive cars and a house that cost you more to live in then you earn.

Unfortunately we live in a society where we are judged based on how we dress, where we live and what we drive. We accumulate debt just to fit in to society. I know a girl whose closet is filled with things she just had to have because a friend or co-worker had them. Many of us are guilty of similar acts. Whenever I think about my complicated life, seldom do I find that health concerns are to blame.

How am I going to pay the rent on a house I can no longer afford? Move to a smaller place with a manageable payment.

What if the closets are too small for all my stuff? Get rid of all that junk, you have too much anyway.

I have discovered that the more material I accumulate, the more complicated my life is. A complicated life does not go hand in hand with inner peace. There came a day when I felt I was at the end of my rope. My family would be as happy in a smaller space. A small car would be more economical than an S.U.V., and I really did not need another pair of shoes.

My friend Nathalee gave up her apartment and moved in with a friend. That allowed her the financial room she needed to save money. My friend Colleen decided that instead of buying Christmas gifts for everyone she knew, she would only buy gifts for the five boys she befriends at a group home in Canada. Her Christmas was less complicated and more enjoyable. Lisa moved from a brand new apartment in Manhattan (with an elevator) to a smaller, older four story walk up so that she could continue living in the neighborhood she loved. She gave up some of the conveniences of the newer place to save a thousand dollars a month.

Of course you do not have to move out of your home or change the face of Christmas to live more simply. There are things you can change right where you are. Go through your closet and your children's closet and give away all those unwanted and unused items. Give them to a women's shelter. With less choices to make in the morning as to what you will wear; you will have more time to meditate and pray. Buy groceries in bulk and save yourself frequent trips to the market. Save your gasoline and bike to work (if you are close enough) or use public transportation. Biking is great exercise and the time you spend on the bus or train can be used for reading a good book (like this one).

Take Action...

Today, Rid yourself of the things in your life that complicate it. Learn to live with less. Live simply.

Journey 34

The Answers You Seek May Already Be Inside You...

I had this urge to seek the advice of a spiritual guru. I felt the need to sit in a yoga position at the feet of an advisor and let him or her tell me everything I needed to know to be a better me. I felt that an entire day with this spiritual know-it-all would be all I needed to be 'cured'. I told a friend about my desire and she reminded me that whenever I spend time alone with God in meditation and prayer, I always get the answers that I need. I was reminded of all the times God spoke to me directly about what I needed or what He needed from me. Why all of a sudden was I looking outside myself for guidance when the answers have been inside me all along?

Every now and then we all need to be reminded of things we already know. Journaling is a good method to use for seeking advice from yourself. What I mean is this: There have been times when I have re-read my journals and discovered something profound I had written months or years before. An example of this is; I had a relationship come to an end. I mourned the loss of the relationship and suffered through a few days of feeling sorry for myself. While going through a journal, I discovered an entry from a few months prior where I had indicated that I needed to end the relationship myself. This person had been draining me for months and I had advised myself (through journaling) that it was time to walk away. That entry caused me to realize that I had been mourning the loss of this person in my life rather than rejoicing, as I should have been. I was seldom myself around this person and with them out of the picture I was free to be myself again.

The wisdom I needed to feel better about the loss of my relationship was inside of me all along. It was the best advice I could have received.

People have sought the advice of spiritual leaders and have found the advice to be beneficial. I thank God that He has given me spiritual ears to hear Him and the intuition to listen to my own gut.

Take Action...

Today, if you have not already done so... START JOURNALING! I always date my journal entries so it gives me an idea of when I had this profound insight. The wealth of information I have found in my journals have been beneficial to me on many occasions. Keeping a journal can be like visiting a therapist or a spiritual advisor, but a lot cheaper.

Journey 35

Pray For Peace…

There are many paths we can choose on our journey toward peace. I have offered the best advice I could throughout the chapters in this book. However nothing you do will make a huge difference in your search for inner peace without actually praying for peace. God is the God of Peace. He is the ultimate source of the very peace we are seeking. Tap into the source. Praying and talking with God is the only way we can ask Him for the guidance we need on this journey.

John 14:27 in the New Living Translation says; "I am leaving you with a gift; peace of mind and heart. And the peace I give is a gift the world cannot give. So don't be troubled or afraid…"That is comforting news coming directly from the mouth of Jesus Himself. The very peace I have been seeking all these years has been at the center of my being all along. I have never known God to make a promise that He did not intend to keep, and if He tells me that He is leaving me with peace, I will take His word on it.

I believe that the wisdom that can be gained from the Tao Te Ching, by Lao Tzu is invaluable and practical; however the peace that I have gained from God is the kind of peace that cannot be attained from any other source.

The power of prayer is an amazing thing. Women have been praying for the health of their children and the longevity of their relationships for many years. We have prayed for our children to come home safely from war, and now we even have to pray that they make it home safely from school. On 9/11 we all prayed for our country. On that same day I was praying desperately for my sister Lisa as she was flying in from New Zealand (her plane was already in the air when the attacks happened). We have seen miracles happen when we pray, lets now pray for peace in our lives and in our country.

Lord God, you said in Your word that You would leave with us the gift of peace, and now we come humbly before You seeking the Source of that peace. We realize today that all the advice that we can gain about finding peace will only work when we go directly to the Source. We ask that as we journey You be the Light on our individual paths. We live in a time of war and turmoil both at home and abroad and we ask now for the peace that surpasses our own understanding. We ask that you give us the strength to keep our heads held high even when our inner peace is challenged. Give us the knowledge to see pass this day and give us the wisdom that we will need for each step along the way. We ask this in the name of Your Son Jesus.

Amen

Take Action...

Today and every day, pray and ask God to accompany you on this journey. Welcome the love He has for you and trust that you can lean on Him along the way.

I wish you an abundance of blessings along your way. Be forever blessed on your journey.

Journey 36

Our Journey Continues...

The end of this book does not indicate the end of our journey. For many of us, the end of this book is the start of our journey. This is the time when we put everything we learned into practice. I was careful to make sure that this book was the perfect size to keep with you to serve as a reminder or a quick reference whenever necessary. To this date I still rely on the wisdom I learned from Victoria Moran's book "Creating a charmed life." I carry the book with me and whenever I need to I can open the book to any chapter and get a little dosage of something special. It is my desire that this special book I put together for you has a similar impact on your life.

It is my prayer that as you read my words and thoughts, that you came to know me and learned a little more about yourself as well. Be encouraged on your journey with the knowledge that you are not on this journey alone. I am grateful to all of you who decided to read this book and join me on my journey. I thank you from my heart. I feel as though I gave birth to this book. God planted this seed in me and I nurtured it, loved it and literally carried it (thank you laptop) with me for nine months. And now as I give birth to this amazing book I pray that you take every word with love just I intended it to be. If you came across a part in the book that made you laugh, then I am pleased to know that. If you came across a part that made you upset with me, then that is the part you need to work on. That particular area is the part that requires your attention.

I have one final "Take Action" for you. Go to your local bookstore and buy a beautiful journal. I want you to write your own book. Add your own chapters giving additional advice to women who are trying to begin their journey. I believe that every woman who enjoys reading is just a pen and paper away from writing her own story. Write me and tell me your story, I would be honored to hear from you.

Thank you for accompanying me on my journey. Be forever blessed on yours.

May God himself, the God of peace, sanctify you through and through. May your whole spirit, soul and body be kept blameless at the coming of our Lord Jesus Christ. The one who calls you is faithful and he will do it.

1 Thessalonians 4:13, Holy Bible

In the Moment...

When I was writing this book, I was warned repeatedly not to write in a way that would be dated. For instance; I was working on the book at the time my grandfather passed away. I wrote something like "My grandfather passed away last week..." my editor told me not to write in that manner because for the person who is reading the book a month or a year later, this event did not just happen. I write in the same manner I speak, so it made it very difficult not to write in that way.

I write this to say, that at this moment I feel compelled to write in this moment. In this moment; we recently elected our first black President. This is very important in my community and perhaps in yours as well. I want to fully experience this moment. In this moment, I recently went hiking in the Grand Canyon, and rafting and wading in the Colorado River. What an experience, one that has to be caught in the moment because pictures do not accurately portray the way I felt in that moment. In this moment I am preparing for my second trip to Alaska and I get to experience it with someone who has never experienced the beauty and magic of that place. In this moment, my children are old enough for me to appreciate their independence and their beautiful personalities: yet not at the age of rebelling. In this moment, John, Travey and Janel still get excited when I come home. In this moment, my Grandmother

Leasie still has the capacity to live alone without assistance, my mother and father are still just a phone call or short drive away and my beautiful Great Dane Abbey is still as active and healthy as ever.

In this moment, I am enjoying every day to the fullest and experiencing things at a level I never could have imagined. I am experiencing love at a level I never knew existed and I am embracing change in my life, in this moment. No doubt, my Editor will cringe at the dated words on this page, but at this moment, I am compelled to write about these things.

Living in the moment and being able to fully appreciate that is a beautiful thing. I came to embrace so many magical things simply because I chose to live in the moment. I do not always live in the moment. There are times that I am still haunted by my past and past hurts. Because this happens, not just to me but others as well, we should be able to appreciate those times when we are living only in the beauty of the moment.

May you embrace - this moment.

www.ingramcontent.com/pod-product-compliance
Lightning Source LLC
Chambersburg PA
CBHW070501100426
42743CB00010B/1713